My Black Swan Calling

Calling

A Poetry Collection

By

Carl Butler

MY BLACK SWAN CALLING

By Carl Butler

First Edition, First Printing
United States of America Catalogue in Publication data is on file with the Library of Congress, Washington DC, USA.

A CIP record of this book is available from the British Library

Author: Carl Butler
Editor: Amanda Jayne Benton
Formatting: Charles Cooper

Published by Elizabeth River Press
Lovettsville, VA, USA
Elizabethriverpress.com

ISBN: 978-1-952818-03-5

Poetry

Carl Butler

FOREWORD

By Carl Butler

My writing is highly inspired by nature and during the lockdown, on one of my walks, a black swan flew overhead with his mate to a nesting site, which I had spent a year trying to find. My patience was rewarded when I finally caught this fantastic event on camera!

A black swan is an unpredictable event that is beyond what is normally expected of a situation and has potentially severe consequences. Black swan events are characterized by their extreme rarity, severe impact, and the widespread insistence that were obvious in hindsight.

I was originally going to do a modern-day Decameron, 100 poems over 100 days during the lockdown. To date, I have written over 1600 in total! So, how appropriate a title, "My Black Swan Calling & other Poems!"

This book of poetry will be a roller coaster ride of personal emotions with my love of nature showcased throughout, with some highly metaphorical poems. Join me on a personal journey through nature and a final chapter, on dark poetry, dedicated to the Dark Poetry Society Facebook group and my fellow co-owner, muse and best friend Amanda Jayne Benton.

Carl Butler

TABLE OF CONTENTS

PRELUDE

DARK POETRY SOCIETY

Vampire desire
Lemonade and cherry red
Sinister ship
Ripper
My friend death
A Tale from the crypt
Re witched
To the hanging tree
No stately ghost
Nox spectrum
Where spirits dwell
The reaping
Banshee
The reapers show
Foe play
Moon curse
Raven heart
The card Game
Fairytale
Sinister
Black Swan Evolution

MY BLACK SWAN

Turn about hiss and shout
From victim to victor
Earthquake off the Richter
Natural disaster
What is coming after?
Your calm is so resplendent
On freedom we're dependant
Show us all how it is done
Despite all odds you've overcome

APRIL 2020

TREES

Standing, reaching, grasping, clawing for the sky
Fingers spread, once naked, now clothed in green
Feet in wet clay so deep, the winds they do defy
But bend or break, the only options to be seen

Springtime jewels of white and pink or cream
Contrast the regimented distanced, standing line
Seen anew awoken, from a frosted winter dream
The gnarled aged skin gives way to smooth and subtle vine

Just one more year of isolation, standing bare
Marking time and seasons with a ring
Showered, suntanned, dried, and dressed to appear
In summers new green, fashionable bling

But all too soon, the green turns brown
As time turns aging decoration, to hues of gold
When at last its cloak comes floating down
The winds whistling through the hair and limbs grew cold

Several hundred years or more, this cycle to continually repeat
Standing sentinel to peace, love, and war
But human contact forces lines to retreat
As life is ended by sharpened axe and tooth set saw

But nature brooks no argument and now
Unbalanced seeking retribution, is her way
A purging need to reap and then re sew
Leaves axe and saw unused and stored away

Millennia may pass for all we know
The sentinels in splendid isolation, once again
And in the spring, new green shoots will show
New life from roots buried and in pain

Seasons cycle through the ages, undisturbed
As saplings don their summer dress anew
As sinews strain and limbs stretch undeterred
A stronger line was formed, dressed, and grew

SHADE AND SILHOUETTE

The passing of the noonday sun, above the tree
Remembers me in shadows blind
No colours can I see
But sun-kissed flowers face the sky
And turn their heads in glee
So while the sun shines all around, only the shadow kisses me

The suns warmth heats the grassy ground
The dried earth powdered brown
My body stays cold and grey
And doesn't make a sound

My solid form, obsidian black
My memories do forget
And shadows touch my stone-cold heart
I am a silhouette

CONTRASTS

Where once sunlight, shared my bed
Now moonlight comes to sleep instead
Once warm and safe in her embrace
Now coldness sits upon her face
The glow that once I saw that day
Now turned to silver, fades away

AYLA

So vivid such, my memories of light
Soft halo shines, the super moon this night
Beneath the oak so sturdy, strong, and true
New shoots grow a gift, to mark your presence in this world, to bring us hope of
future times to spend with you

The moon across the heavens shines tonight
But pales in comparison to your light
Your radiant beauty newly born
Reminds me of the time I've lost and things I've missed, but just your photo gives
me hope reborn

Ayla, you're the halo around the moon
More vibrant than a sun-kissed day in June
Your smiling face is all I need to see
To be a moonstruck fool and know that life will never be the same, but your joyful
countenance, makes me feel free

MEADOWLAND QUILT

Of the meadow and of the tree
A quilt of lilac flows like the sea
Bluebell carpet, bramble, and briar
Dandelions and daisy chains, I long to admire

Locked away so dark and small
Closed in by the concrete walls
Claustrophobic thoughts and guilt
For leaving behind my meadowland quilt

SHADOW FALL

The shadow fall is darker, where the branches meet
The fading sunset light begins, to make a slow retreat
Daytime wildlife slumbers now, as evensong draws near
The velvet veil of night prepared to draw down over here

The fade to black is so intense, the river light is stolen
The orb that is the sun sinks low, red sky turning golden
Now tawny owls do stir and hoot, a weasel scurries past
And playful bats zig-zag around the trees, they move so fast

The river turns an ink-like black, no reflection to be seen
The eerie sounds of night begin, the darkness of a dream
The badger moves out cautiously, to forage through the night
Watched by piercing eyes, nocturnal creatures, hone their sight

And so in this expanse of darkness, nights' cloak envelopes all
Footfall made so slowly home, to avoid a sudden fall
The bible blackness seeps into my bones, before too long
My eyes adjust as best they can, my breathing cold and strong

Heart beats faster in anticipation, of the worst
What lurks within this dark place, could easily be cursed
But logic beats emotion and so my course stays true
To wend my weary way uphill and see the journey through

Soul mates in natural states are never far apart
Limbs entwined the dance begins, but only nature sees it start
There is no time limit to this waltz if only left alone
Watchers stand in awe of them, as their love is clearly shown

Enveloped in a verdant grip, embraced under the sun
The moon and stars look down at night, the dance is never done
Slowly, ever slowly now, two entities are seen
To inch ever closer, as their space becomes dark green

And just as every twirl is meant, for two, to share their Joy
This aging prance goes far deeper, as time rolls slowly by
Until in ages yet to come those two souls merge as one
And so conjoined romance remains as if only just begun

Spare a thought for the natural dancers, as you go walking by
Let their love blossom naturally, do not disturb, Goodbye!

THIS QUIET PLACE

Skull and Bones is all there will be
When they lay me out, by this shady tree
No sunlight, just cold and black
Eyeless sockets staring back

So I come to rest in this place
To think to dream and slow the pace
Lie outstretched and watch the sun
Heavenly peace can be such fun

I come here just to reflect and roam
I know I'm going to die alone
But once I'm gone, I guess we will see
Who will come to visit me?

Lost in thought I sit in the shade
The birdsong music's loudly played
Contemplate how to find myself
Where I've been sitting on the shelf

So lazing in this quiet place
6 feet above my permanent space
The silence of the view I will see
Just the church, headstones, and me

So roam, reflect, relax and stay
Get used to where I'll be one day
Planted near other souls at rest
No fanfare! It's for the best
I decided I'm not going to be
The best-dressed corpse in the cemetery
Chasing money, fame, or wealth
Means nothing compared to sustainable health

Seize the day old Horace said
For in the future we are all dead
Make the most of every day
Don't simply wish your life away

My neighbouring souls have a lot to say
Guess I'll have company on my way
To wherever my next stop maybe
I don't fear death if it catches me

WILD WHITE WOODS

There's a place where I go, in my mind
Where white, silver and green, are frequently seen
Carpeted snowdrops you'll find
And the birch bark is ancient but the leaves are all green

There's a place where I go in my head
Where the wildlife is friendly and comes when I call
I lay on long grass for a bed
And no humans disturb this tranquillity at all

There's a canopy of trees, in my thoughts
With an opening glade, that looks up to the stars
And it lights up, with a silver of sorts
As the moonlight beams down in regular bars

There's a forest right here in my brain
No one can visit it's my happy place
Someone's trying to enter again
Now the white room is back, the wild woods replaced

Jacket bound but free in my psyche
To wander my woods and listen to birdcall
But here in my head is my key
My mind floating free while my body just falls

I'm sheltered from harm with my wits
While they're trying new treatments, to show me I'm mad
But I'm stronger and will never quit
If I'm insane, I'm happy and they are all sad

Now they're trying a drug on my sense
So that I'll admit I'm mentally I'll
And pay some mind recompense
But my wild white wood is with me still

I return to the place in my mind
Where the snowdrops are blooming the rabbits are playing
I haven't really noticed I died
I'm now free in these woods and here I'll be staying...... Goodbye!

MOMENTS

Like the brush of butterfly wings
The eclipse caused by the moon
The comet shooting heavens sky
A sweet caress in June
Real moments are few, exciting, and new treasure them all

True inventions of the mind
Seeing the birth of your first child
Snowfall on Christmas day
Watching orcas in the wild
Real moments are rare, fantastic, and scarce, treasure them all

Like a walk upon the moon
Running barefoot in the grass
A magic symphony composed
Under the waterfall being splashed
Real moments to hold, so bright and so bold, treasure them all

A twin rainbow towering high
When dolphins come to play
Colours beyond compare
Watching dragonflies dance today
Instead of running away, I decided to stay, I would have treasured them all Seeing
swans migrate at dusk
A shadow through the trees
Regale a hero's tale of old
Lilac scent on the breeze
A path not met to live with regret, so treasure them all

NOVELLE

When I walk in these ancient woods
I don't feel so old
The lines in the tree bark are more pronounced than mine
A sign of sturdy wisdom and patience to behold
I stand like a small child against this lofty line

When I tread these ancient paths
Time slows down
My aging limbs seem to regain some youth
In the presence of this elder race, I lose my frown
I sit awhile and search for inner truth

When sitting in their shade, I recall my life
The short span of years I've been allowed
Knowing a few years from now, my end will be nigh
My actions going forward will be proud

When I listen to a conversation, carried in the breeze
These mighty boughs have the knowledge to bestow
Never have we seen times quite as strange as these
But nature will prevail in this we know

When I watch the falling leaves, I don't feel so sad
About my thinning hair and greying beard
Both more signs of wisdom, so I should be glad
My thoughts and actions are now cohered

When I hear the running stream, my heart is filled with joy
Water dancing joyfully in the sun
Recalling loves and losses I gladly bear my Croix
For my autumn days have only just begun

When I see the bluebell carpet and the white starred ridge
I remember long ago when I was a boy
I realize this novella is written unabridged
So seize the opportunity to fly

When those that follow me, walk these woodland paths
Fond memories of me I hope they glean
My trust, pride, and confidence right till the last
When comes the curtain call, the final scene

MEADOWLAND QUILT

Just have to make peace with it all
Before my end, my time to fall
Make sure my life was spent well lived
And for mistakes I've made, I've been forgiven

So my bones they're laid to rest
Dressed up in their Sunday best
To sleep, at last, I'm finally free
There's just the church, headstones, and me

AN HOUR IN THE GARDEN

Sat in the garden surrounded by green
Barefoot in the meadow grass with daisies between, my toes
A haven for butterflies, the birds and the bees
I can just hear a buzzing sound up in the eaves

The sentries are posted, the workers are out
Leave them alone, nothing to worry about
My robins are nesting in the bamboo again
Soon a new clutch of my red breasted friends

Blackbirds and sparrows, great tits and a thrush
Sat amongst nature can be such a rush
The pigeons are cooing, I hear the crows caw
I'm watching a magpie, wishing for one more

After all it is joyful, serene & divine
Just wish I could spend a little more time
The weather is perfect, the zephyr is fresh
A bit of a bite though, should you be nesh

A woodpecker knocked, almost at my front door
Sat in this haven, these days I adore
I savour these moments, whenever I can
My names father nature, a tree hugging fan

MAY 2020

BELTANE FIRE

Fire dance
Begin to prance
Woodland manse
Hypnotic trance

Summer night
Burning light
Ancient right
Mayday delight

Glowing fire
Growing desire
Natural allure
Senses afire

Rhythmic beat
Intensified heat
Souls replete
Spinning feet

Celebrate gods
Renewal rewards
Fertility scored
May queen lured

Green god stood
Shadowed wood
Coupling good
Rite understood
Beltane ode
Musically told
Ritual mold
Success foretold

Forest kept
Goddess swept
Union blessed
Nature's breath

Drumming loud
Chanting sound
Dancing around
Harmony found

Renewal begun
Serious fun
Festivities done
Rising sun

Carl Butler

Blessed day
First of May
Rejoice repay
Renew stay

Beltane fire
Flaming pyre
Ritual sire
Gods retire

OCTOPUS

This tentacle belongs to the Houdini of the sea
A super escapologist, longing to be free
You'll never keep him caged or bound
He leads a lonely life
Intelligent chameleon
Can hide right in plain sight

Takes the shape of rocks or sand
And colour changes too
Can hold tools in its tentacles, just like me and you
Changes its appearance, just like we change our shirts
Can even transform on the move, while its jet propulsion works

Comes in different sizes and many different styles
Some even make a garden, to relax in for a while
But they have some kissing cousins, you never want to meet
Just like the fearsome vampire squid
A monster of the deep

But size does not mean harmless, just like venomous snakes on land
A blue ring octopus will poison you
But he's smaller than your hand
And if you scare an octopus, they have a little trick
They'll squirt water through their siphon, but they'll cover you with ink

It can look amorphous, with no skeleton to break
The only hard part of this guy is his stony parrot beak
So when you see a tentacle coiled up to the end
At the other ends an octopus, a very special friend

YEW AND ME

Bury me by the immortal yew
It's verdant canopy, to guard my bones
Its poison needles straight and true
Its hollow trunk may house my soul

Druids worshipped around this tree
Before the church ever came
Transfer your magic power to me
That I may see again

You stand immortal, evergreen
Gnarled bark wizened with time
Share with me, the sights you've seen
Now I lie here most sublime

And so in death, I meet with you
Your shadow marks my grave
Massive trunk, proud standing yew
Strike a note, on your lyrical stave

Your noble roots embrace my bones
Just as a mother holds her child
Your wisdom great and knowledge old
Helps my soul to smile

Now my ghost can dance with you
Feel the breeze again
The energy pulsates right through
Every fibre of our being
I now share your immortal trance
Staring at the living
Sometimes see the faithful's stance
With their immature misgivings

With seasons turning year on year
I bathe in your fire, berry glow
A standing tree of death, I hear
But I know this is not so

In these seconds of forevermore
My consciousness expands
I've shared the magic of your core
That to root and branch extends

Buried by this ancient tree
Guarded by its canopy
At one with the elements constantly
A union of man and tree

Carl Butler

RELATIVE ROBIN

Seeing you visit once again, old friend
Dressed in your bright red-fronted waistcoat
Receiving the message you calmly send
From a place beyond death, a time so remote
You've visited now and stayed to the summer
Abating my lonely repose and foul humour
Helping me focus on thoughts less sombre
Missing the way you truth, killed the rumours

You sing of renewal and growth through the season
Isolation was never a burden to you
Your love and devotion abound beyond reason
Have served in kind, to help make it through

So sing me a song sweet, red-breasted robin
The tune that my mother would wax by my bed
Call to the heavens from this humble garden
And tell her I'll be visiting her soon, in your stead

Your help to transform my fear and the longing
As my turbulent journey nears the end
I realize now that's it's just a new beginning
Passing on to meet family and friends

Thank you for easing the pain of my passing
Please carry my soul, where you fly oh so high
The dark veil is lifted, my conscience relaxing
My soul has been reborn now I've died

THROUGH MY EYES

If I laid out our memories, end to end
They'd encircle the world with more to spare
Remember the time we became more than friends
We've been through so much, but you know I still care

Back then we had dreams that reached beyond the sun
When did I lose that fire, in your eyes?
So many adventures when our joining begun
Reflect on our lives and our remorseful demise

If I emptied our passion into the wild rolling sea
It couldn't be contained, the world would flood
An emotional wasteland now is all you'll see
If you soul search my eyes, that sparks gone for good

Oh, what times we had when young and carefree!
Wind in our hair, as we travelled the roads
The camping, the riding, just living free
Now I look in the mirror I'm ancient and cold

When the ice came we glowed so hot, it would melt
I remember the times when I worshipped your art
Our stories grew longer than Orion's belt
But now they're just dreams, as our lives grew apart

Our wild abandon, like the storm upon the cliffs
A dangerous dance, but what a romance
The outcome became the four most marvellous gifts
I still see them now, although much time has been lost

The outings, the wanderings, our time by the sea
More precious moments than stars in the sky
Individual jewels so valuable to me
That inspiring river has long since run dry

Such pride we both have in the family we made
Three cowboys and a damsel, in a wild west shoot
Ice cream, fair rides, and carnival parades
Those saplings matured and strengthened their roots

I live with regret at the time spent apart
Missed so much growing, teaching and love
Too late to rewind, no matter how smart
But my love showers like raindrops, from heavens above
Now all grown up with lives of their own
So pleased they've become better people than me
Such are marvellous harvest, from the seeds we have sewn
To a new generation now there are three

THESPIAN SKIES

The overture commences
The stage is newly set
The audience is watching
The cloud actors do their best

As the orchestra crescendos
A rumbling begins
Thunderheads are cleft apart
As the lightning bares its strings

The rains begin their chorus
The winds begin to howl
The curtain's raised abruptly
Grey thespians frown and scowl

This operatic stage show
Is drawing to a close?
Trees wave in their ovation
Moon crescent ends the show

Thunder claps appreciation
In the rolling skies
The stars prepare their encore
As the storm starts its reprise

The heavens part in unison
To reveal the velvet black
Moon s silver soprano song
Star lighting at the back

Then the sound of silence
Suddenly descends
The shows complete
The curtains Dropped
This score has reached the end

THE COTTAGE

There's a quaint old cottage in the country
The roof is thatched, the roads are bumpy
Walls painted white, the timbers black
With several stables at the back
Imagine this rural scene, where the sky is blue and the trees are green

This rural cottage is hidden away
There's a gap in the roof, where some Robins stay
Made a lovely nest this house was truly blessed
To have these lucky birds to stay
When the chicks are born they'll chirp all-day

This cottage has a split stable door
Swings open to reveal a red tile floor
With a pantry alcove and a wood-burning stove
This kitchen smells divine
Herbs, spices, cheese, and wine

The stables tucked to the side
A large green hedge, then a field behind, where the horses gallop and play
One white horse is with a foal today
As they graze the open field
A stabled horse is still concealed

The field lies lined by a bank of trees
That form a green deciduous wood
Where the bluebells dwell and the forest smells
Of fresh flowers and leafy moss
You could wander off and get truly lost

As violet dusk stains the scene
The trees turn black, instead of green
Bats come to play, owls stir for prey
This whole nocturnal scene
A fantasy land has drawn from a dream

A new golden hazy dawn begins
The sun starts to rise and the birds all sing
This rural charm set off the cockerel alarm
As the chickens start their day
The cows roused from slumber, the old fashioned way

Now I leave this cottage by the field
So much happiness has been revealed
I don' know when I can call again
But return to this place I will
Just hope this magic, is alive there still

JUNE 2020

SAY IT WITH FLOWERS

You may say it with flowers
Is that a guilty mental state?
Done something you shouldn't have
Been on an illicit date

A ruse to ease the tension
Placate your darling wife
When you take her flowers
It's just a twisting of the knife.

You may say it with flowers
A gift for mother's day
You moved away some time ago
And never come to stay

You never phone nor text nor write
Don't visit through the year
You'll dump them on her mantle
Then promptly disappear

You may say it with flowers
Well, isn't it too late?
When they're six foot underground
They really can't relate

To their wonderful aroma
Or the dazzling colour scheme
When you take them flowers
You're living in a dream

So don't say it with flowers
Leave them where they are
Appreciate their beauty
Admire them from afar

Stop and Smell the Roses
And see their colour too
Leave them let the wildflowers grow
A tip from me to you

A DAY AT THE BEACH

Twisting, convulsing, and gasping for air
Sweat soaked in agony, just too Ill to swear
Quick get the ventilator, plug this man in
He's on his way out if we can't revive him.

No not another, we're bagging them up
Battlefield tactics, this mentally sucks
Just triage decisions on who lives or dies
A damning result of deceit and pure lies.

Came from the time of our pent up release
First stupid act, just a day on the beach
Met with some friends just to get a quick tan
Sharing a picnic, a bite, and a can.

The danger is over, we've all been let go
Like torrid rivers, to the ocean, we flow
No social distancing, ahh what the hell
Let's have a party, get the neighbours as well.

Well the hospitals fill up, the nurses get tired
The grave diggers love it, they're on golden time
The heat is horrendous, it's 30 degrees
Get those dead bodies into the deep freeze

The doors get re-bolted, but the culprit has escaped
Free to wreak havoc, his wrath will be great
Just wants retribution, for locking him down
He committed his carnage, all over town

The mortuaries fill up, the economy bleeds
Infections are endless, like dandelion seeds
Waft in the wind, who knows where they'll land
A populace thinned, by the wave of a hand

Let off the leash, you're all showing some skin
Transmission central, the rot has set in
Chance of containment, really quite slim
Well f@@@ it, we'll let the best immune system win

TICKING, TICKING, TICKING.

Will, it never stop?
That ever ticking, ticking clock
That metronome inside my head
Could hang upon the wall instead

Will it never, ever yield?
The pumping heart; its rhythm sealed
Inside a cage of bone and flesh
A rhythmic beat, like gears that mesh

Will it never, ever cease?
The thunderheads, their rage increased
And pit a pat, or rat, tat, tat
Those raindrops on the windows tap

Will it never, ever, end?
A blood fueled gushing sound that rends
And tears the fabric of my mind
What to do? I can't decide

Will it never, ever stop?
Will it never, ever cease?
Will the volume, never drop?
Please help, I need release

Will it never, ever stall?
This high pitched noise, this free for all
Buzzing thrumming, humming wires
Or the click, clack rolling of car tyres

Cease or stop or stall or end
One more hour I cannot spend
Clawing, banging at my head
Long for the silence of the dead

Relaxation for my mind
The written words for me provide
The solace for that metered time
My inbuilt clock spins out the rhymes

So whilst I suffer this abuse
At least I have a creative use
Of the feelings so pent up inside
These poetic words flow with pride.

THE DEEPEST CUT

Stood at the cusp of a revolution
Water and tunnels a transport solution
Opened the ways from inland to the sea
A free flow of commerce for all to see.

Canal system worked by a series of locks
A lift or staircases the boats would be blocked
By high wooden gates with a sluice in the side
Moving the water across the divide.

Boats would change level then on they could float
Horse-drawn to start with then fuelled by coal
But the engines moved slowly so not a surprise
The boat's lack of speed became its demise.

Over the years rail and road intervened
A fast pace of life onto which we were weaned
So now it's all fishing and the odd pleasure cruise
Or for narrowboat owners to live on and use.

The wildlife made the canal-side their homes
A wonderful place to peacefully roam
Easily trekking for hours in a day
Or paddling their lengths in an old-fashioned way.

The canals and rivers of England provide
A haven for wildlife to live and to thrive
But remember this story plainly put
The "'navvies" dug out this deepest cut

("For those who don't know **cut** is black country slang for canal")

SQUIRREL SECRETS

The world's most agile burglar
A pirate of the green
Burying his treasure horde
Where sunlight's never seen.

This sailor of the forest
Can scale the smoothest mast
Traverse the woodland sails aloft
Only rarely he'll a vast.

This climber needs no crampons
For his vertical ascent
Sleeps beneath the canopy
Doesn't need a fabric tent.

Quite the comic fellow
Dressed in red or grey
Quite a cunning colour scheme
To blend and hideaway

This acrobatic villain
The master of trapeze
Doesn't use a safety net
When he jumps between the trees

His territory's astounding
His treasure scattered around
Has a magic memory
To retrieve it from the ground

They may be rather skittish
But certainly not shy
Play their games upon the green ignoring passers-by

For when it's time for winter
And the food is scarce to none
He'll dig his store of nuts back up
And take them to his den

Not hot on social distancing
When they winter in their lair
They'll share it with their neighbours
A true family affair

The young are born sightless
3 months in squirrel home
Before their mother kicks them out
And leaves them free to roam

Their front teeth keep on growing
Yet they're a cute and furry sight
Just don't do close and personal
Else you'll get a nasty bite

Now in this little tale, I've told
These are squirrels of the trees
The comic circus acrobats
Of the high wire and trapeze

But other kissing cousins
Live upon the ground
Digging holes and burrowing
Sleeping underground

And of course, we haven't mentioned
The master of the sky
The air-force flying squirrel
Who cannot just jump but glide

I hope this gives some insight
To the rodent of the woods
Don't leave your window open
If you want to keep your nuts

WHAT'S A LIFE WORTH?

A kiss and a cuddle
A trip to the pub
A day with the family
A rave at the club

A day at the seaside
To lounge on the beach
With hundreds of others
Within easy reach

A protest rally
With thousands hemmed in
The next gym session
That luxurious swim

The journey to work
On a tube train or bus
A need to shopping
And empty your purse

Maybe that hairdo
Or a trip to the spar
Barbecue Sunday
Or watch that rock star

Back to your day job
More money to earn
Restart the economy
Send the kids out to learn

STONEHENGE SOLSTICE SLUMBER

I was dreaming, of this summer solstice streaming
Dressed in white and red, with my staff aloft I said
My prayers of thanks, within the standing stones.
As the sun began to wane, I started my refrain
My ode toward the sun, the festivities begin
Dancing through the night, amidst the stones

We danced by firelight, these pyres were flaming bright
The oratory sound and the music playing loud
This festival of thanks was in full swing.
Waiting for the sun, with some adult tactile fun
Or quietly reflecting, on the story that's selected
And listening to spiritual tales of old

To find a spirit guide, sat with arms open wide
Or chanting solstice blessings, taking healing lessons
Waiting for the power of the sun.
Then came that perfect hush, right before the rush
10000 pairs of eyes, look directly at the sky
As the sun peeks past the horizon just before dawn.

Then came a shaft of light, so golden and so bright
Aligned with the headstone, then channelled to its home
In the centre of this temple of the sun.

GOING DOWN

4, 6, 8, 10 metres, more
Fading light, greens take the fore
Other colours, they did fade
As my farewells, I had made

No air to breath in the murky deep
Under pressure, need to sleep
Came then, to my happy place
Travel weightless, as if in space

Air supply, but hard to breathe
I double-check before I leave
Hear my breathing, heavy and hard
From a previous illness, lungs got scarred

Regulate my breathing now
Have to make it last somehow
Just enough to help me see
Where I want my end to be

I know there is no sweet return
But for the ocean, I did yearn
So these memories I will keep
As I fall into the deep

Now 20 metres down, or more
Darkness coming, to the fore
My vision blurs
I cannot see but 10 feet in front of me

Shadows moving out of sight
Corner glimpses in the night
A constant ringing in my ears
Increasing pressure starts to squeeze

Sucking air at faster rates
As it compresses in this state
Down to darker depths, I sink
At 40 metres hard to think

See the images in my mind
Of the family, I've left behind
If all the things that I have done
And the brilliant people, they have become

Heavy breathing in and out
My air supply is almost out
Time to drift off in a dream

To sink into the murky green

Until it becomes as black as night
Sun can't penetrate
There is no light
I hear a distant beeping sound
I realize it should be loud
But I am in another place
I have left this frantic race
A place where at last I'm free

In the deep and calming sea
Still, I sink I'm going down
My conscious mind is shutting down
My eyes open 1 last time

White uniforms are stood inline
The beeping stops
And a sudden click
Time of death 21:56.

TIPPING SWANS

See the tipping swans, glide upon the mere
Plumage shines, snowflakes upon a mirror
Reaching depths mortal eyes can't penetrate
Bottom feed, rear upended, and paddling gait

Social circle, exclusive dining club
Members-only, dinner dress by the pub
Supine necks, black pearl eyes find lunchtime fare
Graceless poor relations, not welcome there

This fine repast served cold, must hit the spot
Now comes time to play, stretch and ease the knots
Stretch angelic wings, no intent to fly
A vision to behold, by passers-by
To radiate such beauty, so serene
Belies this comic feeding, stylish scene

JULY 2020

WHERE THE MONSTERS ARE

Looking back in history
Through records, we can plainly see
Through both fact and fantasy
Where the monsters were

From werewolves, vampires, and ghouls
To mad science and its evil tools
And human evils act so cruel
The monsters rested there

Then blind dictatorships were formed
Resulting in two worldwide wars
Deaths and suffering and so much more
That's where the monsters were

But in 2020 we should be ashamed
For monster status, we have gained
For evil doings, we've proclaimed
This is where the monsters are

Untold deaths caused by omission
Many more by indecision
Hard-won freedoms back in prison
This is where the monsters roam

A viral killer on the loose
Talks of solutions so obtuse
We have no heroes they're no use
The monsters in our homes

Psycho actions and madness reigns
What we've lost can't be regained
And nature's very fabric maimed
Can you see the monster's yet?

No use looking beneath the bed
Nor the cupboard above your head
Try the wardrobe there instead

Check the mirror then
You'll see the monster's back again
Behind your eyes is where they stay
Your actions let them out to play

SOLITARY SOLDIER

A beacon in the darkness
The never-ending night
Brighter than the moonlight
And the stars in distant sight

Standing on the rock face
Vigilant, straight, and true
I am the only guiding force
Equipped to guide you through

Reach up to the heavens
Tower above the sea
Withstand the stormy battering
As waves roll onto me

A solitary soldier
My duty shall remain
To see brave souls away from the port
And guide them back again

You see from the horizon
My light sweeps across the bay
I warn of rocks and hidden reefs
My beam says to stay away

Revolving in the darkness
From atop this white stone tower
My singular existence
Provides life-saving power

I have a lonely keeper
To keep me company
My life is spent in service
As he will service me

I am a serving lighthouse
Upon the headland stood
Standing here for all to see
And radiating good

I am a sailor's protector
And guardian of the sea
No recognition do I seek
As ships sail across the sea

I watch lonely the horizon
And hear the ocean swell
Dream of the underwater world
The place where mermaids dwell

So if you ever see me passing
And see my moonlight show
Please stay a safe distance but by all means, say hello!

UPROOTED

My roots were shallow, my spirit hollow
Circumstances laid me flat
My growth was stunted, my seeding halted
Leaves lay on the forest mat

My storm swept boughs, once home to crows
Now grudgingly, in the earth, they lie
My offspring distant, deep-rooted and innocent
Not knowing whether I'd lived or died

My will lies dormant, my soul in torment
Stuck in limbo, nowhere to turn
My limbs but hunks, of dried-out wood
In a forest fire, my soul may burn

Alone and lifeless, I suffer in silence
No one knows I'm even here
Whilst it's chilling, my life's not finished
Of that I know I'm perfectly clear

Where I lie, just left to die
New life starts to spring up out of me
Insects use me and crawl right through me
Through the bark and body of this tree

New moss treads and ivy spreads
Clothing my nakedness in green
New shoots growing new trees are forming
My legacy, at last, is seen

STARSTRUCK

I looked into obsidian
That blackest pitch that night bestows
Where even shadows cannot dance
Is there even the slightest chance?

I started into the void
Flightless and limitless devoid
A black without substance
To penetrate perchance

Looking at the black
Now silver pinpricks staring back
Constellations beam
Celestial bodies glow and gleam

Staring at the stars
Wanting wishing twinkling star
Searching for your grace
That unique vision out of place

On the horizon far
There at last you shooting star
Your purposeful travail
Through heavens ocean singly sail

Join you in my mind
Seek the knowledge you may find
Your' fleeting sojourn here
Stains the sky with a single tear

Comet of the night
Celestial coma trailing bright
I lie in awe of you
Of where you've been and what you've viewed

A send you my thoughts, hopes and dreams
Carry them safely spread them widely
And just be...

THE CHAINSAW MASSACRE

Walking the canal path one evening I saw
No glimpsed is the word through a mist so raw
The rev of an engine a pitched growl
Interrupted only by the screech of an owl

Narrowboats moored for the night
No one around as the cabin lights burned bright
Sun sank behind the clouds scene turned grey
But these horrific sights still with me today
A headless torso minus any limbs
They were strewn about like Child playthings
This massacre well underway
Chain teeth biting and chewing away

The visored assassin simply smiled and said
When I've finished the body I'll start on the head
I'll slash and cut and saw and maim
These lifeless limbs won't seem the same

My head imagined those silent screams
Nightmarish contortions in my dreams
Lifeblood slashed and poured away
A sum of this macabre scene today

When I screamed "Where's that body from?"
Ahhh it had fallen there, in the woods my son
I saw an eagle within this form
Just had to set it free from the shroud it had worn

So I've cut and hewn and sawn again
The shape now emerged can you see it, my friend
I know your concern you've expressed it to me
But I assure you this was, a long-dead tree

TWO FINGERS TO SOCIETY

A colleague died just yesterday
From the virus, he passed away
Yet people walk around without a care
Just pretend it isn't there

We'll all go out its all ok
Just wear a mask keep it at bay
Of this bullshit, I've had enough
Yes isolation was very tough

But helped to get the death toll down
But cost too much so they've shut it down
Now you've all gone berserk
While the virus in the shadows lurks

Too late to prevent the spread
Let the councils sort it out instead
We want the dough and don't care how
We'll ignore the science now

The clock is ticking it's a sin
My the best immune system win
From what I hear and what I see
It's just 2 fingers, too society

TALKING HEADS

Are they all just talking head's?
These people on TV
All this media melodrama
Is really crimping me

Where are the social statements?
The emotional epithet
You've all got lost in Emmerdale
Or EastEnders better yet (not)

Well I don't watch television
Its morphine for the brain
My eyes would just start streaming
Bleeding with bad pain

All this plastic acting
May have people hooked
But I'd sooner sit down
And read another book

Or if I have some time free
I might pick up a pen
And write some flowing poetry
This really is my Zen

Journeying with nature
Or deepest darkest thoughts
Commenting on history
Or quick rhyming retorts

Words are quick words are clean
Words are cutting words are mean
Rhythm flowing meters keen
Iambic pentameter Shakespeare's dream

Or choking out trochees and setting the scene
Changing the rhythm to get the full effect
Build your excitement. "Are we there yet?"

Well we've gone in a circle
What's left to be said?
I might not be a poet
But I'm definitely no talking head

WRECKERS

Black as pitch and thick as tar
The fog sat heavily on the cove
Trees wuthering in the storm
As rain lashed down through the grove

Down the steep and rocky steps
From the headland to the shore
Drenched Sowesta and wader boots
As I heard that creaking sore
A light upon the headland shone
A beacon burning bright
But right atop the craggy reefs
Where there should be no light

The beacon meant to safely guide
The sailing ships to shore
Now removed and doused right out
Decoy light was to the fore

Like a moth to flame the ship it came
Then listed on the reef
Guts ripped out by wrathful winds
That drove onto jagged teeth

No chance for the sailing crew
Not many left alive
But those who managed a trip to shore
By morning they will have died

Murder foul and looting too
These villagers intent
Wreckers all, this ship and crew
To Davy Jones' locker sent

Quickly now these figures worked
And rigged a salvage line
Barrels boxes bales and sacks
Was the booty they required
Rum and ale and spices too
And even treasure chests
Then spied the captain with a gun
But a sword stove in his chest

Not a sailor left alive
Kill everyone you see
The penalty for wrecking death
So I'd rather them than me

Now get this haul back through the caves
Through smugglers cove, we go
We'll divvy up the spoils anon
When no one needs to know

But get up off this blasted beach
Afore the soldiers get on down
Else it's for the gallows tree
I'll head to some strange unforgiving town

Well sing to me sea shanties boys
As I work through every hold
Clearing cargo by the crate
And a horde of assayed gold

You'll have food this winter
Whilst it may be rough and plain
The blasted ship's new owner
Can put through an insurance claim
But that's not where this stormy tale
Would ever really end
For every year at midnight
That rocky crag doth rend

Now the ghosts of ship and crew
Haunt this savage cove
And tales are sung now every year
Of the shipwreck, the wreckers drove

AUGUST 2020

Carl Butler

THIS HEART BETRAYED

How should be remembered, this heart betrayed
Plucked from my very bosom, by your hand
Loved, then cast aside, as you cruelly strayed
Whilst kept my aching soul locked on remand
Indiscretions mounted, tallied yet you stayed
Creature comforts always part of your demand

How should be remembered these souls lament
Weeping blood from open wounds so hard to staunch
Whilst thought those pained affections were heaven sent
Just manoeuvers as your lust campaign was launched
Now upon my rendered soul, your devils' mark beset
Resulting from your actions so debauched

With wanton disregard, you left with no regret
And a horde of snide remarks of tasks avouched.
My shattered petal soul, I slowly mend and brace
Wove with strands of iron, my defence in place

HOW LONG THE NIGHT?

How long the night?
Till you seal your kiss with destiny
How deep the dark?
To swallow the star of infinity

How black the soul?
That feeds the flame of infamy
How foul the deed?
To stain your life with ignominy

How stained the seed,
That spreads your canker lustingly
How sharp the knife?
That marks your kills disgustingly

How long the night?
Before the dawn, you're afraid to see
How tight the noose?
That has you hanging from the tree

WOODEN WARRIOR

In my travels, once I saw
A wooden warrior with axe and sword
A wooden shield on his left arm
A stalwart look of utter calm

An anvil jaw and staring eyes
Then all at once to my surprise
This valiant knight made a sound
A rasping bass like the rumbling ground

Sword in hand I crossed the land
Came ashore on foreign sands
Ready for surprise attacks
My shield prepared an axe at my back

A valiant army came ashore
From Viking long-ships in days of yore
Raiding parties started west
We had our gods and we were blessed

Encountered foe but bested all
Our courage held by our heroes call
Valhalla s feasting halls ahead
Should we meet our heroes' death?

To fight for honour bravely gained
Our legacy our noble names
Warriors and farmers both
Swore allegiance and sacred oath

To our liege and one true king
Brave old tales of which we sing
But one day in one small town
A wizard stood in garb and gown

With Hawthorne staff and hat of grey
A long whispering beard that blew and swayed
Barring now our onward path
Said with force you shall not pass

Well of course this got us mad
So we went on the attack
But one by one we were struck down
By this tattered tramp in this barren town

Then, at last, stood only me
He looked me up and down with glee
Chanted something merrily

Then turned my bones into a tree

No Valhalla nor feast for me
Now doomed to spend eternity
In this field of enmity
A mind enslaved inside a tree
A wooden knight for all to see
To scorn and jest and beat on me
For target practise I've been used
My skin is wood but my hearts abused

As I've aged become confused
Can't remember many truths
Only one of import now
How to end this lifeless show

A warrior's end I need to take
One last fight I need to make
Help me lift this cursed thrall
Then cut me down let me fall

With sword in hand and a trusty shield
All my secrets now revealed
Odin grant me strength somehow
To meet this warrior and his bow

Notch an arrow, Sir let it go
You'll pierce my heart then blood will flow
I stand here with my broken sword
Valhalla my just reward

No further words now as I fell
To that young archer William Tell

EMERALD POOL

This emerald pool where the air is cool
The willows weep so gently
Trees reach so high to grasp the sky
Their shadows long and stately

Deep in shade near wood and glade
This treasure is so well hidden
On muggy days with a rippling haze
These pools so good to swim in

The waterfalls cascade and call
Free-flowing to this green mere
Their freshened haze and sonar daze
Makes me glad to be here

Insects peace their courtship dance
With airborne high precision
Upon the morn of a passing storm
Lights refracted like a prism

Herons fish take their tasty dish
From trench, carp, and barbell
Ducks whiffle down to this bejewelled crown
This story done now ends well

A ROCK AND A SOFT PLACE

Time moves on so slow to see
For the sea, the sky, the sand, and me
The lapping waves that lick my brow
Cool my head with their ebb and flow

The golden glinting of the sun
Arcs gently south, the day's work done
Leaves golden hues and copper streaks
As the tide comes in and the moons released

The waves play, gently haunting songs
As they roll ashore, just one by one
A lone seagull soars across the painted sky
The clouds draped in bronze just standing by

Darker now this sea of night
A deepened blue with flecks of white
Flotsam gathers at the shore
Jet-some joins them, now there's more

And all the while the tide returns
But soon I know that it will turn
And at the dying of the light
My silhouette stands proud tonight

Where it has for ages done
And as it will force more
So slowly edging with the sand
As the beach slowly shifts at seas command

But upon the cusp of land and sea
Those movements are too slow to sea
As Canute of old sat at the shore
Knowing what he had in store

The moons tidal grasp may not be mocked
But at least I'm just a rock

CASTAWAY

And the skies began to weep
For all their tears they failed to keep
Locked up in their cloud bound hearts
The tempest tearing them apart
The riptide rushed along the sea
Faster than the eye can see
Graphite, charcoal blue, and black
These angry clouds hold nothing back
And the wind-borne dervish feigns an attack
Into this course, I blindly tack
No navigating now
The waves come crashing over the prow
If snagged upon the reef
My windswept heart will come to grief
My charted course belayed
Tempers now becoming frayed
Alone for all these years
The sum of some conflicting fears
When finally, 'becalmed'
Egregious waves have spared me harm
And yet I shall decay
A loveless broken castaway

GOLDEN EYES

I looked into the eyes of a killer
Anthracite black with a golden sheen
Face to face with a ripper
When the moon was obscured
No shadows to see

The rapier blades of a hunter
Predacious stare with focussed intent
The stealth and grace of a ninja
Glides through the shade
Of the Cimmerian woods

In awe of swift wings swooped to slaughter
Feathered and sleek talons and beak
The tufted ears of a marauders
Dives for its prey shredded in sway

The tracking skills of a stalker
Soars through the skies with large disk-shaped eyes
This bird is a screecher, not a squawker
Right before dawn mouse ripped and torn

Nocturnal grace of this reaper
Dealer of death and master of stealth
Sibylline flight of this killer
These acts are not foul it's a huge eagle owl
Looked up at this shape of the ripper
Shadow fell black right before the attack

Those golden eyes, watch nocturnal skies
Stare down its prize, swoop with surprise
The animal dies, a prey in demise
An eagle owl reprise, off she flies

BRIDGE OF SIGHS

In the misty glade bedecked in shade
Reflected in the mere
The emerald hues bejewelled with dew
Belied a rising fear

Now these verdant trees a perfect frieze
Beyond the bowing path
Hid a place an awful space
Where wraiths would scream and a laugh

A haunted dell where spirits dwell
And ghosts are haunting still
And if you stray to their lair
They'll drain you of your will

These spirits dance an ethereal trace
Will overcome your mind
And once they've fed you'll end up dead
And you will join their kind

With mouth agape there's no escape
They'll hear your silent screams
Invade your head thankfully in bed
It's all just a bad dream…..

SEPTEMBER 2020

ODE TO THE MOON

You are the moon to my bright star
I worship you, but from afar
You wax and wane as mood frequents
Yet never waver in your intent

My northern star will be your guide
For your contention, to decide
I twinkle pale against your light
Dimmed by your beauty, every night.

Before the dawn had kissed the sky
This silver moon has winked her eye
Dazzled night owls in their flight
What a surreal mercurial sight

RAGING SWAN

Beauteous in her anger
Grace incarnate in her rage
Protective wings of comfort
Flap wildly on this stage
This very changing current
With circumstances new
The season's change
New threats emerge
But she will see them through

With total concentration
She will protect her growing brood
From predators that come her way
Or try to steal her food
This most elegant of dancers
Is a natural warrior born
Underneath a calm demeanour
She will rage against the scorn

This queen rules by a succession
And she'll choose a mate for life
They'll face many untold dangers
And go through hardship, pain, and strife
Even to her partner
She can be rather rough
But it's just her temperament
She has to be so tough

Yet loyalty and loving
Are these beauty's traits
And while she may be masterful
She rarely makes mistakes
Look upon her angelic form
And any heart would yield
Just remember she's a shield maiden
Who can battle in the field?

So when you feel her anger
Sometimes untold wrath
Please respect her territory
For this is all she has.

FALLEN IDOLS

Remembrance in the courtyard or cenotaphs of old
Some sit and watch from parapets
In church eaves, a look so cold
In museums, they're painted vivid hues
Like silver blue and gold
And everyone stands silently their stories to be told

Yet sandstone and marble shapes are all they'll ever be
If you want to know their legacy then turn to poetry
Living words and turns of phrase for everyone to see
These are penned monuments to go down in history

The giant's shoulders on whom we stand to write our work each day
Had broken dreams and nightmares and with lunacy, they'd play
Unrequited love and lust in life's tragedies held sway
In black and white infused with blood these fallen idols stay

From heady arcane manuscripts to Facebook groups today
The plethora of written works deal with many shades of grey
A poet's words are living proof they boldly sought the fray
Conquered many fearsome foes, weaving words in the melee

Don't miss this part of history, a waxing poet's works
Broken down experience and thought revealing quirks
These pages filled with love and hate
Where pangs of hope still lurk
So say your piece and write it down
This duty does not shirk

AUTUMN'S GOLD

Autumn's gold is precious
That fleeting Midas touch
Before the winter strips its boughs
And leaves are turned to dust

The knowledge of the ages
Contained within one leaf
The winds blow strong and blustery
And then she comes to grief

A reservoir of feelings
Contained within these trees
Now life's decay has stripped away
And brought me to my knees

Seeds now spread and dormant
Overwintered in their graves
When leaves carpet the woodland floor
Then we shall do the same.

BATS IN THE BELFREY

I am the night's enigma
I am leather and I am lace
It's rather nice to meet you
I have a furry face

I hang around on bridges
In attics or town
I have this silly habit
Of hanging upside down

I use echolocation
To find my way around
I actually can see quite well
But use the sight of sound

A few high pitched
Squeaks and squeals
And I know where to go
The sun drops past the horizon
I can put on quite a show

I'm quite the aeronaut
An aerial display
When I'm chasing insects
I'll zig-zag away

I must be pulling several gees
With my tight twists and turns
I am a night-time flyer
And more agile than any birds

Whilst I'm rather small and cute
And fly around with ease
Humans don't like me much
They think I spread disease

But I'm not a nuisance
If you leave me alone
Stop chopping down the trees
And I'll vacate your home

In June I'll have my family
In any local roost
We are a maternal colony
To give the kids a boost

Don't need our boyfriends
Until it's time to mate

So don't want them underfoot
Whilst in this maternal state

It's not until September when
We start to get quite fresh
Then I'll let him back again
I can be rather niche

Have to wrap up nice and warm
To stay active in the night
Otherwise, I slow right down
And that's not very bright
I'm rather small and furry
I'd got into your hand
I cover quite a territory
The skies at my command

As the only flying mammal
I'm really quite unique
I've never really learned to talk
But boy I sure can squeak

Once the autumn over and
Winter comes around
I look for a new roosting site
To sleep the winter out

I have a 9 monthly calendar
Sleep through the other three
Whether hanging in a belfry
Or stuck inside a tree

Once it gets to April
After sleeping safe and sound
I'm getting rather hungry
And start flying around

I have a healthy appetite
When I feed through the night
3000 insects I can eat
On a healthy diet
My big ears help me find them
While flying in mid-air
And independent hand wings
Help me catch them there

So if you ever see me
When the sun goes down
Remember I'm quite friendly

Even in the town

Unless I am vampire bat
A bat of some renown
Now that's a different animal
For I survive on blood

I'll drink on horse or cow alike
Or humans if I could
It takes only 30 minutes
For me to have my fill
And unlike in the movies
I never ever kill

If I'm in your bedroom
And you're sleeping in your pit
You wake up and see me
You'll already have been bit

And should I carry rabies
Which bats may sometimes do?
You'd better see a doctor
Before rabies sees to you

But I rarely feast on human blood
As you might believe
I am not Count Dracula
I'm sure you'll be relieved

MY SUNSHINE FIELD

Rarer than yellow my joy, till we talked
Then through a dreamy sunshine field, I walked

SOLITUDE

And in the solitude of silence
And the spilling of the sand
Now the hourglass is broken
And the metronome at hand

The rapture now behind me
All I have left in life
Are the footprints on the beach?
And the outcome of my strife

MIDWAY TO WINTER

Midway to winter
Autumn finished soon
Leaves soon stripped from naked boughs
And there's only half a moon

The clouds devour her greedily
She showed her face to soon
Stars blacked out from this canvassed art
It's the wind whistling that tune

A 40mph concerto
Sends shivers through my bones
I have to seek some sanctuary
As I'm miles away from home

The sea is rough in temperament
With her rolling diva waves
Crashing against the headland
And into newly formed caves

The trees wave in the cemetery
And the grass grows on the graves
The cows lie down in the field today
As they anticipate the rain

What a thrilling season
That will so quickly end
Then winter snows
And the north wind blows.
While I'm camping in the tent

The clouds are black and pendulous
Yet such a welcome sight
At least they're quite gregarious
So I won't be alone tonight

My moon has gone for this evening
Or maybe now for life
I see her up there leaving
And she's looking rather trite

The stars have gone from the firmament
All colours drained away
I'm not sure what to do
While I'm waiting for the day

I certainly can't sleep now
So I may write the night away

With wildlife all around the camp
And bats that squeak and sway

Sudden scurries in the dark
As the wolves just start to croon
The howls are rather lonely
As they echo beneath the moon

But just as there is no one to hear
So no one listens to me
Alone again my weary thoughts
The steel grey clouds for company

And one lone star shone fleetingly
Oblivion then for me to see

CRIMSON ARCHITECTS

Blood our medium of choice
Sometimes stippled on white canvas
Contrasting tones within the voice
A reminder of our sacrifice

Words built on words in red
Mixed with graphite and cerebral sweat
Torn and tattered we are led
By the litany of the dead

Towers of crimson fashioned anew
Mortared with pieces of a heart
Those shattered slithers piercing through
Foundations laid the ramparts grew

Sweat and blood on every page
Stigmata coined at every turn
Every coupled word and phrase
Tied with the decaying string of age

When at last the castle built
On tortured minds and lack of sleep
Built from lust and love and grief
A breathless sigh, a life released

So praise the crimson architects
Whose verse adorns our very flesh
Emotions poured with fervoured zest
Their ending phrase their last request

SNOWFLAKE

A fleeting fractal in the noonday sun
Fingerprints on a windscreen run
Such beauty and innocence captured there
Snow white fragility laid out bare

Cold and crisp six-sided trip
From the heaven, you float, twist, and sit
Upon the floor and walls and trees
Or float diagonally in the breeze

Dreamcatcher delicate soul entrapped
Crystalline ice with a water wrap
Once the surface touched you turn to tears
Perfect symmetry belies the years

Cold your reception and crisp to touch
Natural perfection yet melts too much
Why such beauty dare not be seen
By naked eye, an angelic sheen

A lattice framework is so distinct
Precipitated you slowly sink
Your brothers and sisters pile up more
Leaving drifts to form great mounds in store

Delightful dancers twirl and twist
Floating frolics with a sudden tryst
Lattice lovers so delicately kiss
Upon an ice-cold winter, your touch is bliss

OCTOBER 2020

RIVER OF INFINITY

Nature changes seasons as we would turn the sluice gate wheel
Omnipotence within, her all encompassed grasp
Wrapped in golden rustic charm
Life flows and eddies beyond her sluice
Tumultuous change to see
Then suddenly it rights itself
And calmly heads to the sea
Like driftwood left to find its way
While leaves rain on its wayward path
Temporary maybe its stall
Against protruding obstacles in its sight
But time and current flow soon turn
And leave them standing in its wake
As the season's turn
So I will reach the sea
There to reach like-minded souls
From the river of infinity

PERFECTIONIST

I'm not looking for perfection
I would not know where to start
All that I have ever known
Is a yearning from the heart

I see people for who they are
Not who they're supposed to be
And I've seen so many broken lives
Just struggle to be free

I'm not looking for perfection
Let me be rather crass
I'd sooner have a friendship
With a real pain in the arse

Life should not be boring
All sighs and pregnant pause
Get those demons dancing
And bouncing off the walls

I'm not looking for perfection
Soul mates being the wrong word
When you stop to look at poets lives
It's really quite absurd

No soul could live through shared loves
Such heartbreak, death, and pain
Dust off the crumbled rubble
And get right up again

I'm not looking for perfection
Because, God I am a mess!
For 99 percent of the human race
I really can't care less

Their stupid blundering, greedy ways
Meant a long time ago I was through
But decide to carry on
Now my heart is set on you

HOLDING A GHOST

Curled up again in sorrow with my pillow in my arms
A repeated situation as it can't resist my charms
Sideways supplication and I'm holding out my palms
I wanted some sweet music but got Liszt instead of Brahms

Handled the rejection, yes I took it and stayed calm
Whilst I didn't understand, it may it soothe me like a balm
Felt like shovelled shit that got scraped up from the farm
My insomnia works overtime, no need for an alarm

Some days close to exploding, I must be rapidly disarmed
The emotion that still tortures me, that rage leaves me becalmed
I reach out with my writings hoping the subject may be charmed
But still, it's just a ghost I reach, I'm haunted but forearmed

FORGED

We forge our lives with hammer blows
In fiery pits and full bellows
Quench our mettle till it's done
Just look at what we have become.

Formed in presses rolled on mills
Our characters have been instilled
By heavy toil in the industry
Concrete flags in the big city

Tempered steel and vice-like grip
Fermented ale to well-parched lips
Helmet lamps lowered down in lifts
To the hell that is the pit

So turn the wheels of industry
Not a blade of grass to see
Never a bird nor verdant tree
We formed the bars of misery

Live to work not work to live
An early grave is all they give
Maybe a watch to mark your time
For a servile lifetime what a crime

No fresh clean air nor nature's views
Verdant trees and worldly truths
She gives and takes but never uses
And to her kin never refuses

So lose yourself upon a trail
It matters not you will not fail
To find the answers that you seek
Listen calmly and let her speak

WAVES

Like a crashing wave against the cliffs
Came the torrent of your kisses
The freshest rain on dew starved leaves
Your caresses charge my very being
Static electricity rolls through my limbs, so easily

Transmitted by your liquid love
The tempest from the skies above
We clash as land and sea in storm
Our passions overflow to form
Such combined power and sensual bliss
I'd give my all, for one night of this

SHIP IN A BOTTLE

My darkened dream of loneliness
On the clipper ship of solitude
She carries heartbreak and regret
In her overflowing cargo hold

Emptiness fills her canvas sails
She cuts through placid murky seas
Her keel runs keen through despair's depths
Becalmed by lethargy's vacant breeze

Grey horizons haunt me here
As I wish for seas of blue
And raspberry ripple candy skies
The freshest memories of you
Longing to tarry on your shores
Oasis bound my hope renewed
Your soothing sand beneath my feed
Shaded caress upon my head

But the anguished ocean holds me here
Her flaccid sails and broken mast
Leave this ship bereft of life
A soulless sky of steely cast

These well-charted waters have no end
Night and day I plumb their depths
Fathoms marking out my pain
In the endless ocean of regret

I spy your green and fragrant land
Rose-tinted spyglass to my eye
Wish the wind to carry me
Beneath a rolling cloudy sky

But there is no beach no anchor point
This vessel languishing in time
A bottled ship on painted seas
My message is hidden in this rhyme

AN AUTUMN AIR SHOW

It was a late autumn day
With a chill in the air
The squirrels at play
But the weather was fair

Sun shining away
And the sky mainly blue
Came the aerial display
Of birds passing through

First came the bombers
Formed in a V
A passage of geese
In their wedge flying free

Out on their wings
And equally strong
Came another contingent
A squadron of swans

After their passage
The fighters appear
The swallow test pilots
We're dive-bombing their peers

Swifts performing acrobat
Like grey lighting streaks
With a rat, tat, tat
Of the woodpecker's beaks

Next came the Hercules
Of this little display
All camouflaged
Confederates in grey

Flying in formation
Exceedingly rare
At graceful close quarters
12 herons were there

Along all the phone wires
The birds stood and stared
Magpies and blackbirds
And crows undeterred

Watching these migrants
Much misunderstood
Some leaving the country

Others leaving the wood

Even the seagulls
Flew inland today
Just to take part
In this airborne display
Rather haphazard
Their antics quite crass
Fighting each other in the skies
And on the grass

Then as the sun sank
And the shadows came back
A chorus of birdsong
Precedes an attack

Eagles and buzzards
And night owls out two
Hunting for prey
In the fields, what a view!

SAMHAIN BLUE

Of rarest hue, your countenance will shine
Through wisps of grey a picture so divine
This Samhain eve a sight so seldom seen
Your reverence staring down on Halloween

And the red god Mars sends crimson tinted notes
Bone fires reddened glow to tame the ghosts
Keep Samhain spirits locked beyond the veil
And all the monstrous things duly curtailed

The hallowed, misty, hazy Oracle
6 dozen years and 4 elapsed to call
Upon this Samhain hunters night revealed
Shadowed haunting cosmic light concealed
From druid times this fateful time was due
Samhain evening full moon shining blue

NOVEMBER 2020

FOREVER DOESN'T CARE

I can't promise you forever
As forever does not need us
We are irrelevant to him
Just a passing whim

I can promise you devotion
Till I can breathe no more
Till in the ground, I'm sleeping
My lifetime and no more

I only ask forbearance
And just a little love
I'll worship you more than the moon
And the twinkling stars above

These seconds of forever
The ones that I can give
These and my heart I hand to you
We can count together, whilst we live
When the hourglass has emptied
The final grain will break the glass
Just remember that I loved you
Right up until the last

A LAST GOODBYE

Fleeting, slowly beating
The snow-capped heart
In winter's hearth
The sun, my face is heating

Pastel, the last handful
Our heads will weep
Prior winter sleep
And the snow drifts fill this landfall

Golden, sight to beholden
The peaks give rise
To a mawed surprise
A zephyr, so softly spoken

Mountains, on you we are counting
Through this deep freeze
Steel your shoulders, please
Against the violent storm-force shouting

Melting, snows in springtime
To crimson hues
We will push right through
The bluebells peel their ring time

Sighing, at last, we are dying
One last goodbye
We kiss the sky
Our floral spirits flying

GHOSTWRITER

Sleep, no damn sleep
When shall it be replete?
I have a manuscript to complete
Yet my mind will not repeat
The words I need

Write, you're so damn right
Don't give up tonight
This becomes your legacy
There's nothing else I know, you see
For I am you and you are me
The ghost of future passing

Live, and fall in love
There is no passion up above
Find your soul and let it go
To play gently with another
Bare your heart, don't keep it covered
Some years until you pass
Make this one the love that lasts

Please, allow me to release
From these bonds of pure obscurity
The past lives that abjured me
I've paid penance for my sins
If hell-bound tell me, let me in
To the secret beyond the grave
After all, it's all I crave

Write, into the night
This is your salvation, get it right
Don't take a slight, your futures bright
Just reach for the one you need
Destiny will intercede
To give you some happy years
And your name lives on

Once you've disappeared from view.
It isn't you, it is you two
I say adieu

POPPY FIELDS

An autumn day, a tranquil scene
A pastel blue that slips between
Those rolling clouds, above the fields
Green and lush, the death concealed

Poppy red for miles and miles
The blood was shed, it was so revolting
This scene of the war concealed
Beneath the lushness of Flanders fields

The blood that soaks into these fields
Nourishing, this flower revealed
A symbol of remembrance
Of all these tragic circumstances

The loss of loved ones in their graves
Forgotten bones from bygone days
Bloodshed from two world wars
And of course from many more

The carnage caused by governments
Who cannot simply be content
To cooperate but fight instead
Led to millions lying dead

So when you see the poppy red
For your freedoms, soldiers bled
And gave their lives for the country's cause
Remember them with sad remorse

For they fought to keep us free
From the yoke of brutality
Yet look upon what we've become
At the going down of the sun

ARMISTICE DAY

The time that was marked by the whistling of shells
The explosions of destruction
And the sounding of death knells
On the 11th of November time suddenly stood still

That was when the killing stopped
The silence carried through
Whilst I wasn't there upon those bloody killing fields
I dream about those atrocities that the poetry revealed

Accounts from Wilfred Owen, John McRae, and Rupert Brooke
Bring home the red of poppy fields
And what the soldiers undertook

So in honour of that silence as the gun smoke slowly cleared
Sun shining in the trenches and the ever falling tears
Please observe the silence as we hear those big ben chimes
2 minutes at 11 am is remembrance armistice time.

AGING (CINQUAIN)

Aging
Life decaying
Every muscle aching
Memories are slowly fading
Crumbling

ASHES

My ashes will be scattered to the winds
Cast mournfully upon an ocean breeze
To float away, perchance sink to its depths
Where I lay down, at last, my passion breathes

Stifled in this life to the waters I now flow
Adrift, yet in a state of reverie
Deep and dark in this wonderment I know
Rid of life's burdens, I am surely free

For so damned long has this world suffered pain
From man's irrevocable selfish disease
When the floods and fires have this land reclaimed
I can flow with tidal currents, at ease

There is no sadness in my passing away
Shed tears for mankind's ultimate disdain

CABIN IN THE WILDERNESS

Lost in my own wilderness
Where no tracks are ever seen
No rescuers can seek me out
But this place is so serene

No need for roads and byways
Nor even tracks and trails
The landscapes formed within my head
And all that that entails

I have my share of wildlife
To keep me company
They wander in and saunter out
At will, they are all free

I have a wildflower garden
And herbs grow by the door
My range looks like an Aga
And there is strip wood on the floor

It's a tidy looking cabin
With a panoramic view
But you will never find it
Even if you flew

It's weatherproof and cosy
And built for fireside chats
All the animals get along
And there are both dogs and cats

We never go out hunting
So the food is a meagre fare
But to see each season's beauty
Is just a constant love affair

The birds are most familiar
And squirrels nest inside the walls
Bees produce their honey
In the eaves above the hall

I even have some fruit bats
Hanging from the roof
They dance about in eventide
In the day they are quite aloof

With all these creature comforts
I could never be alone
I now wait for the one soulmate
With whom I will share my home.

FAT FURBAG (For Amanda Jayne Benton)

A rather regal looking cat
Snacks too much, a little fat
A fur ball curled up in black and white
Who sleeps all day and plays all night

Washes clean those furry paws
But sometimes, he'll forget the claws
Mostly they are tucked away
Saves them for an angry day

Plays placidly with his treat mouse
Barely wanders out of the house
Eats those treats before his bed
At 4 am, wants to be fed

Meows and scratches till you wake
Spoilt for choice, which one to take
Meat or fish, he's not too sure
Changing tastes make you procure

Different food to suit his whim
But you really have a bond with him
He is your favourite company
However, annoying he may be

You love him, as he's so cute
Even when he's in pursuit
Of Betty puss his feline friend
Of all the cats she could befriend

She chose Kato for her mate
Or at least they've been on many dates
But late at night, he makes a scene
When he's pawing in a dream

But either way, you love him so
And never will you let him go
He is your King Kato

A ROYAL WEDDING

I'm just the dumb waiter at the wedding
Royalty have flocked here to the ball
The king and queen betrothed and now their wedding
Dinner jacketed footmen fill the hall

Cautious coots in dinner suits arrive here
But the snow-white regalia reign supreme
Courtiers are toasting at the fountain
Whilst the royal mating dance gets quite extreme

Wildfowl quack and hiss approval
Leaf confetti lines the floor
Magpies gather up the silver
Whilst grey-suited seagulls bow their heads and squawk

The courtiers line up with emotion
Hearts formed from feathered sublime necks
Trumpet call to herald this devotion
And then frivolity ensues with friendly pecks

A rainbow forms the lover's archway
Way up above the canopy of green
Narrowboats sound off horns of approval
This surely was a joyous wedding scene

DECEMBER 2020

ICE

A rolling sheet of cold that is so extreme
Carves a path through mountains, never seen
A power to render forests barren white
Crystalline and crushing, slow-motion day and night

To an ocean vast this ice flows ever slowly
Sundering the bedrock as it goes
Then suddenly, it meets that waters start
Then pushes ever onward, as it calves and sheers apart

LONELY

In the wilds, it can be lonesome
For a nomad, wild and free
Wandering the hillsides
Through meadow-grass and tree

No time for self-reflection
Just howling at the moon
A little introspection
Then the winter comes too soon

Padding through the snowdrifts
The prey is getting near
A Lone wolf must be careful
When stalking adult deer

Antlers sharp and pointed
Can rip one stem to stern
A clean kill is exciting
But takes much time to learn

Once I have truly feasted
To the lakeside, I will go
Time to quench that hunter's thirst
Then on and on I go

Travelling Oh so softly
A ghost that is never seen
I gaze again at my reflection
In the waters glassy sheen

Realize how lonely
These last few years became
But life within a wolf pack
Would never be the same

I cannot follow orders
And as an alpha, I'm too tame
Maybe I'll meet a she-wolf
And rear some cubs again

But that just summer dreaming
Not meant for winters depths
These next few months
It's hard to live and many meet their deaths

Head now solely focused
On all the tasks in hand
I creep into the shadows
With all the stealth at my command

Brave the winter snowstorm
Battered tired and worn
I make it through another night
And live to see the dawn

VIRAL VERSE

Homeless avoided like they've got some disease
Single parents walking with their kids, ill at ease
Come away Kathy, from the air that he breathes
Your mother went to heaven, no one heard her pleas

Social divide has widened like some tectonic shift
Such a fearful atmosphere it won't seem to lift
A hazy fog of nothingness a hunger driven void
Masked and gloved we walk alone, with contact to avoid

In the war we came together, in this peace we are wrent apart
If only the short-sighted, had kept lockdown from the start
Prejudice and bigotry and panic have ensued
We mourn the dead our hearts have bled, through conflicted attitudes

Open up, no shut it down, the roundabout goes ever round
Until attishoo, we all fall down
Can you hear that silent breathing sound?
That's the latest strain that we have found.

More infections have got round
We take the strain of this new strain
This ninja mutant struck again
Are we insane? It's not to blame
It has a focus needs to gain

Many hosts to replicate
Pass it on and duplicate.
This stop-start process was just great
To let it thrive and then mutate

It mutated fast, well quite a blast
Through the clarion call, of the vaccine wall
Its all-out war, yet no one saw
The guerrilla tactics it has installed.

To thrive and grow, well hope you know!
I'm nowhere near the vaccine show
They don't even know if it will work
This mutant strain is such hard work
In the meantime, it's just berserk

The walking dead just hop on trains
Some sad advantage hoped to gain
From the south, they fled
Their trails have led, too many potential Northern dead

The virus fed and grew and grew
Passed on blindly by all of you
Can't stay away, just had to play!
Queued in shops while kids just played and school displayed
A lack of sense as mothers chatted by the fence
No distance hence, the recompense
Where the hell is common sense?

RAGE

A fit of rage comes over me
When I see what man has done to thee
Polar region's once pristine
Barren rock can now be seen

Wildlife dying by the score
Hunger; famine; drowning and more
Rising seas and melting snow
Soon there will be nowhere else to go

Should I shed my sorrows tears?
It would become a stream of fears
To raise the water level more
Engulf the land, swallow the shore

So keep my anger and my wrath
Help to walk a different path
Conservation is the way
Get eco-friendly now today...

WINTER SOLSTICE DAWN

To be a raven on the wing
Circling, soaring on the winds
Fingers spread, to catch the sun
As the solstice dawning has begun

To be a songbird in full flight
As Stonehenge focuses the light
The birthing of another year
A sense of freedom flowing here

To be a creature of the night
From sundown till this dawning light
Even I would stray from slumber
To see the New Year birthed in comfort

The standing stones just stand and stare
Like time and change were never there
To mark the years their only care
Consequences we all share

Yet humans donned in yellow vests
Dare to mar the dawn's request
Its breath of life to us bestowed
This New Year's gift of rebirth is shown

If only we had been shown
The tranquillity these stones have known

WINTER DINING

Woven web a silken lattice
Dripping with dewdrops from the morn
Adept after years of practice
That spider worked from dusk till dawn

"Oh no!" she shrieked, wind blew colder
Brave arachnid getting bolder
Walked upon a white web of ice
Taut wires now strung across this vice

Built To keep the insects captive
This spindly spider knows her source
Plans to dine on her meat-filled course
In winter snows, quite adaptive

Frozen dessert will taste quite nice
And ice-cold water drink of choice.

KILLER

I'm a 6-tonne hunting machine
26 feet, hungry and lean
The most social of animals you've ever seen
With razor teeth both sharp and keen
My saw tooth grin and Colgate smile
A giant dolphin set to beguile
The bonds we form are very strong
Our pods cohered by falsetto song
We dance and play in the ocean blue
But our iron jaws can bite clean through
We'll eat seals and calves of baleen whales too
Even dolphins we will hunt and chew
Some like fish and chase the shoals
Swim both temperate seas and icy cold
Our two-tone form like shadows fall
Communicating by our calls

Wrangle prey with stark precision
When hunting food we've no inhibitions
Apex predators are we
The lions of the rolling seas
We are orca killer whales
With dorsal fin and flukes for tails
We will jump and breach and laugh and play
Get our females in the family way

Yes you guessed it we are mammals too
Birth live babes like humans do
Our seaborne crèche protects our young
Never a doubt we all belong
And work together for our kin
And share the spoils that we may win
When you see these torpedoes in black and white
Don't be alarmed or gasp in fright

In the wild they may hunt meat
But humans don't make tasty treats
They'll leave us be without a care
So let's leave them to breed and share
Their marine predatory lives
Sung like Angel's, with teeth like knives

BEAVER MOON

Beaver
See her?
The moon of industry
The light that shines she's so divine
Let the work of man and beast continue long into, the cold and blackened night
Building dams and building bridges
Sawing trees from forest ridges
Block the water still the flow
Just another one to go
Yet her presence
Controls the flow
Of the tide
Even when
She hides
Away

JANUARY 2021

BLACKSMITH

Your absence, I captured and fed to the furnace
And little by little, I wrought its shape
With hammer and anvil, I worked on it daily
Till armour is made and a helm to the nape

I fashioned a sword, I felt it so keenly
I have also a shield, to strengthen my wall
Never again will my heart be seen clearly
I fashioned a lockbox, armour-plated it all

STORY

I wrote myself into the story in your bleakest hour
To nurture and water and watch you flower
Once fully bloomed, well-rooted and strong
You can tear out this page, put it where it belongs
Where you have discarded my heart!

SUNDAY LUNCH

The bells are ringing, the choir has been singing
I'm in a church doorway, on Christmas day
The weather, it's raining, off the rooftops it's draining
My sleeping bag is wet, I did not come to pray

I walk around the corner, quite soon I'll be warmer
A dinner, a shower, a bed for the night
So cold and lonely, homeless, if only!
My Christmas gift, somebody cared for tonight

To the soup kitchen, the staff on a mission
To serve us our lunches, from 6 feet away
Did I mention the virus, it's not very nice because
Worse than our looks, it keeps people at bay

A huge Christmas dinner, roast lunch for this sinner
Roast beef and veg, roast potatoes so hot
Sit down to eat, just forget my wet feet,
It's just so damned filling, this meal hit the spot

I eat with such gusto, yet tomorrow I must go
After my shower, I will sleep overnight.
So just after sunrise, from my cot bed, I arise,
Head back to the streets, to where I don't know

So cold and lonely, homeless if only!
More people cared, we would be dry overnight

WEEP FOR ME

When the wuthering, stops briefly
The trees are bare and sleepy
The willow, dank and weepy
As the river meanders on

The ground is white and crispy
I'm walking rather briskly
On the ice, that's rather risky
But I bravely soldier on

The storm restarts abruptly
Snow falls in a flurry
I start to worry
As the flakes, keep on and on

The cold is stark and bitter
I really am no quitter
But I start to shake and shiver
And I'm trudging blindly on

This tempest, more ferocious
The weather, most atrocious
Maybe I'm precocious
But I still must carry on

The drifts are quickly mounting
All caution, I am flouting
Can't consider now re-routing
I must slowly struggle on

All tracks are disappearing
The blizzard now is screaming
It's all that I am hearing
Now I cannot carry on
I slump down, in exhaustion
I should have used more caution
My sight suffers distortion
As hypothermia s begun

In snow, I sit there smothered
Soon completely covered
There's no way to recover
I will soon be dead and gone

I'm not sure what I am missing
A robin is just sitting
As into death, I'm slipping
My soul just carries on

That bird, so resolutely
Simply hops, right up to me
Says rest, now prematurely
Takes my soul, and then he's gone
And so am I!

TANKA

A most subtle shade
Those cheeks retained through the eve
Silver kissed ruby
With those luscious lips like wine
Intoxicating extremes
Made sweeter by the morning

CORVUS CARRION CROW

This aerial display
Midnight amidst the day
No squeaking hawk
Nor harrowed harriers
No stranded ocean
Aircraft carrier
These are the intelligentsia
Precision skills
Pure elementia
Irridescent
And so theatrical
A magic moment
Sung like a madrigal
That murder done
With razors' talons
Those beaks of steel
Will brook no challenge
Deathlike fingers
Disperse the air
We are the crows
In death we share

VIRUS

Last year we caught a virus
Like a spider, it sat down beside us
It curdled that whey
When it came out to play
Now 6 feet and a mask are desirous

ADRIFT

Adrift, in the languid lake of circumstance
Anchor broke and sunk beneath the mere
Relentless tears, which filled this empty vast expanse
No solace found, just one all-consuming grave

Broken on the rocks, that surround its
Barren shore
A thousand cuts of consequence, my map of fears
Endless trepidation, now am I going to float once more
Or drown, under the weighted yoke of years

FEBRUARY 2021

MY MOON

She came to visit me today
In her cold mercurial way
Kissed my cheek as I dared peek
Through the white window frame

She crooned
Her hunger barely kept at bay
For this night only she will stay
From this dark room, she pierced the gloom
I was held within her sway

She smiled
Those moonbeams danced along
As I heard her silver tongue
Enchanting me, entrancing me
What more can I say?

She left
Just before the morning broke
That golden sun had just awoken
A chorus heard of morning birds
But for another year
She has gone away!

UNKNOWN POET

Here lies the unknown poet
He waged battles for his art
His pen was used so mightily
In all manner of regard

A people's poet through and through
He gladly gave it all
Regardless of the censorship
So sad he had to fall

For him, there is no poets' pew
Nor star upon the wall
No caravan nor vain salute
Nor wake to feed them all

His words were ever powerful
Many captured in his thrall
But still, he is buried in a box
Now no one comes to call

His last words now his epitaph
Are etched upon his grave
For this and social justice
His life he gladly gave

A soul so freed from lifelong pain
As he exited life's stage
He did not leave without a fight
That battle sorely raged

Once I'm gone, will I be forgiven?
All the sins to which l was blindly driven
On my tombstone indelibly riven
Rest in peace after a life, long striven

THE WEIGHT

I bore the unrelenting weight of circumstance
Shoulders set to numb the pain of every stumbled step
Became immune to every random
Occurrence
Grim-faced Atlas' provides this raw lament

A time, frozen through glass, shards have pierced my heart
The burden ever heavy, of this constant shifting load
This camel seeking water in a desert ever parched
Trudged through blinding heat and ever numbing cold

Seeking little respite, but a break must surely come
That final straw piled upon this strained and laden back
Losing sight of reason, why this journey had begun
I get a sinking feeling as I step through drifting sands

A journey not completed yet now impossible to end
Stranded in the wilderness to what depths shall I descend?
And yet as those circumstances should transpire
With no respite a further weight, the moon did I acquire
On buckled knees, my sinews strain, my god when I retire
All of me is spent and yet I have but selfless desire

FUSED

A heart once frozen
In summers gleam, began to thaw
But on winter's cold return
Became glass, its edges raw

Transformed by alchemy it seems
By betrayal lust and lies
An obsidian shade replaced this heart
Now darkly it resides

Further heat and further rage
Compressed this darkest black
Till fused with coal and sudden formed
Is diamond shining back?

No harm befalls this priceless jewel
It takes the sharpest blade
Faceted the light shines through
With no impression made

No tales of woe or pleas for love
Affect this crystal heart
Now cold for an eternity
A jewel that stands apart

SELFISH

Just another selfish story
Of a race that fails to think
The human tribe in all its glory
Why not just let it sink?

Beneath the weight of its ignorance
Like the titanic sank before
Maybe we deserve a fate
Similar to the dinosaur

We care not for nature
In fact, we do it harm
View in disgust these pictures
They'll cause you such alarm

The earth is just our trash bin
To throw out what we please
Nothing can cure stupidity
No matter what the pleas

Look for that mighty meteor
Or the fading of the sun
The earth will be much healthier
With its tenacious plague long gone

THREE SEASONS OF LOVE

Summer is the illusion
Bright and shiny, long days and balmy nights
No wrong is done in summer
Senses are ensnared and our imperfections are clothed in green
Or hidden by blinding sun and candyfloss clouds

Autumn, the mirror of spring
Once new life sheds, in a fanfare of gold
It is a highly burnished shield of bronze
All coloured hues are copper tinged
And that elusive pot to which we race
At the rainbow's end, too soon has waned

With winter whites and graphite skies
Equally as hard to grasp
One scooped up prize, simply melts and runs away
Even on the coldest day
Like the heart fearing the shock of warmth

Withdraws behind its ring of steel
Secrets never to be revealed
As the imperfections on the ground
Are lost beneath the snow

And yet from here approaching spring
Comforted with white blankets
Cuddled by cloudy skies
Nourished by the falling tears of nature's dismay comes new life

The heavy-headed snowdrops
Dew splashed and innocent
On fragile stems shrug off their winter cold coat
Become the most beautiful carpet ever seen
Before the bluebells ring

The blue and white, a carpet of unending delight is laid upon the forest floor
A place for picnics and romance
In this ever-changing circumstantial world

I invite you to heal with me and bind those cracks, use my dead heart as spare parts
to bring yours back to life
Scarred but beating, feeling, loving
My exsanguination, a small price to pay
For you, I gladly consider it spent

WOLF MOON

From the edge of the world, I saw you
That far off distant glow
I simply couldn't resist you
But your love I could not know

Still, we were so distant
Forever far apart
Me a wolf in wintertime
You the brightest star

Galaxies pale around you
When you reach your brightest sheen
Not even sunshine can confound you
In this midnight tragic scene

I padded to the highest peak
Just to steal a kiss
A footing so precarious
Things almost went amiss

Trees stood bare in silhouette
Bowing at your grace
The tide below, singing your praise
As shore bound it did race

All that's left for me to do
Is serenade and croon
And so my darling debutante
I'm howling, at the moon

BRIDGE

As this skyway between two bridges spans
All thunderheads and cheerless snow-filled clouds
Relentlessly swells like full-flowing tides
Sending fractals gaily dancing to the ground

HEARTBREAK

A heartbroken so many times
It shattered to the floor
Handle very carefully it is poisoned to the core
Sharp as Sheffield steel and barbed with
Blood red hooks
Wear kid gloves and show restraint, it is sharper than it looks

Betrayal sent striations through its rubied whole
Now where once emotion, lives a void
A tainted hole
These fragile fleeting facet gleaming
Fragments feeling sore
Jagged edged and festering their nerves exposed and raw

To ex-lovers and ex-friends, I've nothing left to give
I've walked away from everything
I survive but never live
A solitary sentient, damned to purgatory
Self-imposing penance
Whilst conversing with the trees

THE ADDICT

It's just a hobby I say again
As I pick up that blasted pen
That ink feels just so sublime
I watch the curves in every line
That sexy black
Like fishnet tights
Wrapped around those silken thighs
Those golden words
I pour and melt
Every syllable keenly felt
The passion rising to the fore
As I write a line I need some more
I need this fix
I cannot stop
Need the high
Can't face the drop
Half past 2 then 3 then 4
I'm still writing
Pen some more
A literate me with your tongue
Those silver syllables can't go wrong
I need this now I need your prize
What's between those poetic lines?
Oh goddess I'm about to come
One last full stop
Now am I done?
Not a chance I'm up for more
My hand may cramp
But I'll endure
Write a sonnet
Then two more
Epic stanzas
Three then four
Then several more
Way beyond the light of dawn
My eyes blood read my vision blurred
Am I really that absurd?
Need a fix
Yes just one more
I really am a poetry whore!

MARCH 2021

MUSE

Should I genuflect for you my gentle muse?
A radiance I can never bear to lose
An emerald amongst this myriad of green
A ruby thrust amidst this wild and wondrous scene

Through your eyes, time slows swiftly to a crawl
Birds surround us, enchanted by your call
Beating wings, a hummingbird's I can count
As we lay twixt these mere moments on the ground

Lost forever in those depthless limpid pools
Moonstruck I am both the jester and the fool
Hand in hand skip twixt raindrops as they fall
Today I lived a lifetime, maybe more.

Wingless words take flight by your sweet charms
Time's shifting sands stood still between your heartbeats
In my arms.

DAMS AND BRIDGES

One hundred eager beavers
Could never build this dam
Bridges have their cantilevers
Built by architect and man
Both have their own stress relievers
Great pressure to withstand
With such a weight upon my shoulders
Should I give a damn?

Steel, stone and concrete, firm foundations
Driven deep into the land
Mortared, trowelled, bolted, dowelled
Constructed by skilled hands
Stand the weathering of ages
But this I understand
This construction counts for naught
If built on shifting sands

Your steel, my bone your concrete, skin
Muscled joints that lie between
Life's stresses tell from toil and strain
Do dams and bridges feel my pain?

Your span, my arms are open wide
I have the humility, not pride
If to spend time with me, you should decide
In my heart, a place you may reside

WILL

Will this veil lift like a dawning?
When I'm lying close to death
Will I hear the birdsong calling?
As I'm taking my last breath
Will the cosmic stars all shine for me?
As I prepare for my repose
Will loving eyes shed tears for me?
Too much to presuppose

Will the sky turn from black to red to blue?
As I fade from grey to black
Will there be some final act?
Now I'm never coming back
Will someone's love sustain me?
Through the darkest night of all
Will you sit with me till morning?
When I heed the raven's call

With you there, I can face this fate
To fade with no reprise
To see a glimpse of heaven
In those loving perfect eyes

But if alone this fateful day
Then frantic war I'll wage
Heaven will never take me
As it won't handle all my rage

Even death will be somewhat circumspect
As he tries to reap my soul
My lust for life is way too strong
To give up because I'm old

So I write my final will
Set in black and white
All I ask please sit with me
Kiss me goodbye that night

ALBATROSS

Feeling like an albatross
With a pair of broken wings
A mobile that is hung aloft
By worn and threadbare strings

Looking upon perfection
With vain hope still, I cling
Salt stained tears well in my eyes
Relentlessly they sting

LACHRYMOSE (Acrostic)

Liquid born of misery
Ampules of salt taste like the sea
Cascade soulfully, wet and slippery
Heavily they flow so freely

Repeatedly flowing languidly
Yearning for some sympathy
Moments of needing empathy
Of such a great intensity

Sorrowful this protestation
Emotion crystallised in tears' creation

PERFECTION

You cannot hold perfection
Neither with the eye nor with the hand
An ethereal projection
It is water, it is sand

Shifting with the desert breeze
Or tempted by the moon
What once was a fair goddess?
Soon becomes a sun-scorched dune

Statues feign perfection
And for centuries may stand
Hidden flaws beyond detection
Break to strata, rock, and sand.

Stories feign perfection
With every silken word
Yet left dust bound upon a shelf
Their beauty is unheard

Poetry is perfection
For emotion is its key
Just like mother-nature
It has timeless empathy

And so it can be written
But never can be held
For it exists inside the soul
A spirit never quelled

PASSIONATE CHESS

Feel static through your fingertips
In pouring rain kiss ruby lips
Feel those smooth curvaceous hips
Get lost in wilderness eyes

Smell the scent of wind kissed hair
Locked inside your infinite stare
Look my love my soul is bare
I'm lost in depthless eyes

Taste the fruit of sunshine skin
Your smile could make a gargoyle grin
To serenade you love birds sing
Inside those starlit eyes

Take you to the oldest tree
I sink obediently to my knees
Feel my passion gently tease
Those hungry sparkling eyes

Then this bold knight shall rise at last
Your ladies favour round this lance
Nothing now is left to chance
I'm lost in bedroom eyes

Drawing water from the well
The tide will rage the river swell
A ride to heaven where you dwell
Behind angelic eyes

The game is spent the moves are done
Laid on the grass beneath the sun
Mate is checked the race is run
Stare into sapphire eyes

THE JAB

The jab, in the lab, is a really small prick
Once I had it, I felt a little sick
Back to the car and sat inside
'Wait 15 minutes before you can drive'
'You may get some symptoms a little like the flu
But don't worry they'll soon pass through'

Now the invaders have set up camp
What's more, I gave them a helping hand
By 9 pm I can't see much
My head is banging, hot to the touch
Temperature has gone through the roof
Joints are aching, feel aloof
Just so damned tired I had to sleep
And sleep, sleep, and sleep

The next morning went to get busy
Off the bed wow just went dizzy
Kidneys hurting need a wee
Can't grab the door in front of me
Throats now sore and glands are swollen
Eyes like piss holes in the snow
Streaming tears all down my face
Drinking water, can't keep pace

Feel my chest now constant pain
Mucus running down my drains.
Went to sleep and slept some more
Feeling drained now to the core
Sheets are wet with all that sweat
But in the evening, it got worse yet
Thought it might get some reprieve
But now it's getting hard to breathe

Oh well it's only for 1 night
After all, they said I'll be alright
Wasn't it a harmless jab?
When it was tested in a lab

MORE THAN THE SKY IS BLUE

To have wants and needs
To love, to bleed
Is human
To feel, to give
To err, forgive
Is human.

I long to feel alive once more
Experience what love has in store.
Above all the need to breathe
Is human.

To want the sun upon my face
To hold your hand, just any place
Is human
To linger in a warm caress
Feel silken skin beneath a dress
Is human

I am the sum of my desires
When did existence douse these fires?
To cherish hold and kiss my love
Is human

But when the sun should raise its head
It shines onto an empty bed
That's too human.
And too true.
The reason why more than the sky is blue.

MEADOWLAND GUILT

(A continuation Of Meadowland Quilt)

Of the meadow and the tree
Quilt of lilac flows like the sea
Bluebell carpet bramble and briar
Dandelions and daisy chains I admire

Locked away so dark and small
Closed in by the concrete walls
Claustrophobic thoughts and guilt
For leaving behind my meadowland quilt

Keys now turned and locks released
Rush to see my meadowland fleece
Diggers defiled that springtime quilt
Corporations feel no guilt

The populace can now roam free
To visit field and spring and tree
Yet be spoiling treasures is their way
Nature breathed whilst we were locked away

Lachrymose I am and miss that quilt
A lake formed from the tears I spilled

NO MORNINGS AFTER

Some old men miss that morning feeling
Its consequences most revealing
In their youth spent time concealing
That tent pole pointing at the ceiling

Some seek porn hub for the answer
Or the latest greatest male enhancer
Maybe blue pills? Oh Viagra
Without the pole, there is no dancer

Of misspent youth so often dreaming
When often accidents came streaming
Embarrassed looks and that wry smile beaming
The aftermath of that sticky feeling

To reminisce is life's great pleasure
Self-satisfaction such a treasure
Men take for granted at their leisure
But all at once no rule to measure

When the back is aching bones are creaking
Bladder control is slowly weakening
Fluids start to seep, they're leaking
Comfort in their old age seeking

Can they fix it once it's broken?
Of this malady so rarely spoken
More should be completely open
Just maybe it can be re-awoken

CRESCENDO

Starting as a whisper
Barely hear it speak
A voice calls from the darkness
Laconic, low and weak.

But its tempo rising
It echoes in my head
My frustration unsurprising
As I'm lying here in bed

Voices getting louder
This nightmare is no dream
My mind starts to flounder
A fish caught in midstream

Succumb to this crescendo
That's raging in my mind
There is no innuendo
To all else I am blind

Do it do it do it now
The voices scream and cry
Painstakingly I write words down
Another poem, born to die

CARL

My Charles Atlas seal of approval
It passed its sell-by date
But those gleaming eyes that mesmerised
Are still in a fine state
They say to look into someone's eyes
You see into their soul
Tell me
What do you see there?
Is there anything I should know?

Sure I am intelligent
But I have no common sense
I have no wealth to speak of
Just work to pay the rent
Not much to look at these days
My handsome days long gone
I speak to trees, have dodgy knees
Can't stand the summer sun
Now I'm quite the loner
Preferring solitude
As my mind, it tends to wander
People think I'm being rude

I'm still a lot stronger than I know
And quiet isn't me
And snoring like a freight train
Well, doesn't bother me
So here I am sat all alone
I'm talking to myself
At least I've got my faculties
And reasonable health
I write some damn good poetry
At least that's what I'm told
I really don't like censorship
And some are rather bold

Now that lockdown's ending
All those interrupted lives
Can go back to their loved ones
While me,
I'll just survive
Done it alone for 8 years
Hope for maybe 10 years more
But who knows in this day and age
What the future has in store

I have both love and loyalty

It has nowhere to go
So I guess I'll keep it in a jar
Where the tea bags used to go
I'm penning this rhyme off the cuff
I really don't know why
I guess we are just emotional
Me, myself, and I

THE SAME, ONLY DIFFERENT

Almost a year since I fell head over heels for that woman I knew, I was destined to be with
I guess this is the truest of tragedies and in the dark, counting stars, with not even the moon for company
I can do nothing but either write or shed a tear and I'm long past crying

I am that same person you felt drawn to all those months ago
The one you had a connection to
And you didn't want to go
The wanting with Friday chats well into the night
Taking about everything beneath the cold starlight.

I am the same person, you couldn't wait to meet
The one who you even allowed to massage your dainty feet
And yet I feel I must shoulder all the blame
For I fell in love with you
So I am different, but the same.

I had to write this down because, in the mirror, I have changed
Still never-ending stamina, in anything that I'm engaged
I'm the constant running bunny
Whose batteries never die?
Just remember that when someday
You phone me up to cry.

Yes my mobility is limited, but I work hard at what I do
And I always put you first, whatever things come to
I'm so sorry after all these months you can't just turn round and say
I accept you just for who you are
Instead, you shy away

I love you more, I love you still and that will never change
If friendship is what you have for me then that's the part I'll have to play
You are the one I've searched for and thought I'd never find
I'm so flooded with emotion and you're always on my mind

This is now the only time I will put this in a verse
Frantic to get my walls back up
My future life is cursed
Some loveless years and loneliness
To this, I'm now resigned
We will both miss out on just so much
But those boundaries you defined
Remember when you need me, I will still be here
When you don't, just let me know and I will sadly disappear

BLACK SWAN CALLING

Is that a wedge of angels flying high
Light bringer straining at their snow bound head
Stygian silhouette in azure sky
Once fell from grace but leading in their stead

Dauntless black with fiery beak of red
Graphite marks like scales on swarthy wings
Due deference shown not hesitance nor dread
With soldier perfect timing, this ensemble sings

Obsidian I see you fly from sight
Unto where I know not but I will search
Your calling brings a portent to my life
Your history and meaning I research

Like opals you are of the rarest kind
Like questing for the holy grail, your likeness I must find
As our fates are intertwined

DARK POETRY SOCIETY

VAMPIRE DESIRE

I am darkness, never ending night
I am seduction, spin to dizzy heights
As your blood seeps from your veins
And you climax, with pleasures pain
I'm your lover and your death
You will crave me, with your last breath
I will not break your beating heart
I'll stop it dead!

LEMONADE AND CHERRY RED

Well the maid, made, lemonade with frosted cakes
To the master's bedroom, she did take
Of something else he would partake
And that was a big mistake

Knife in hand to cut the cake
She slipped in the blade, with no mistake
The lemonade now cherry red
And he's drip drying by the bed

Crimson hand up to the arm
Should have set off an alarm
But she's walking up the garden path
Our prim and proper psychopath

And now, that taste for lemonade
And the crimson cakes, that were displayed
She left this old boy's innards splayed
For she no longer had to be a slave

But now she has the taste for death
Fills her with joy, with every breath
Cascade of crimson behind the eyes
Where the soul is bare and truth resides

Cherry red she paints her lips
Fishnet stockings and charming wit
Drinking vodka and lemonade
A flash of the thigh when a victims played

Offering to share her cakes
The boys all make the same mistake
Thinking that their luck is in
And the night will end in sin

But of course, their lucks run out
Blood will gush as fluids spurt
She collects her samples in a jar
When they come, they've gone too far

Been led right up the garden path
She's had her way and the last laugh
This night of lust will be your last
With this prim and proper psychopath

SINISTER SHIP

A sinister seaside tale, on a dark and stormy night
The mist cloaked harbour veiled, so, no penetrating light
The buoy bell loudly clanged, as that fog so thick and dank
A distant siren sang, from the foul night cold and rank

À ship sailed into port, its mizzenmast sheared through
Sails tattered and torn, as it limped slowly into view
An eerie silence fell, like a curtain drawn by hand,
A ghostly ocean swell drove this broken ship to land

Sudden seagulls flapped their wings, as a flock they took to flight
Some terrifying thing had them sorely spooked this night
As she listed hard to port, creaked and ground to halt
No crew of any sort, neither captain nor old sea salt

A deck bereft of life holds empty in the gloom
The remnants of a fight, as we scaled this floating tomb
Suddenly, purposefully, slowly, I and my fellow shipmates descended the steps,
What foul thing had momentarily taken hold of our senses?

As we went, a dread so deep and woeful, fearsome visions tricked our feeble minds
A sadness lone and sorrowful, of a despairing leaden kind
The Captain's cabin loomed, a leviathan in the dark
A sense of utter doom, bitter bleak and stark

As we breached the coffin door, some 15 bodies lay
Mutilated all, and rotting with decay
 Some foul and sinister fate, befell these men tonight
This listing, crypted crate, held a stomach sickening sight

Suddenly a howl, or a rather guttural growl
And all at once, the demons struck, with murders oh so foul
Crewmen turned on crewmen, a madness gripped the men
A bloody violent brawl began, but swiftly did it end

I had but seconds to escape, as I bounded up the steps
Jumped overboard this cursed ship, as I launched, from its tilting deck
 All the crew were hacked and cut, knifed by each other's hand
This sickness deadly and rife has now assumed command

I ran and ran in madness, in horror and torment
Like a dervish, a man possessed, at a pace, I'd not relent
 Entered the deserted town, limping with one shattered knee
But grabbed the fireman's axe right down, went on a killing spree
Now here we leave this seaside tale, of sinister intent
Of how the sickness came to town and the massacre it rent

RIPPER

The fog came down in London town
A night to never linger
A shadow walked or maybe stalked
His footsteps moving quicker

The lady turned looked quite concerned
And soon a look of terror
A ghastly task her face a mask
Frozen in abject horror

Blade in hand, blood in demand
His hand came out and gripped her
Oh no! She croaked, as he cut her throat
My name is Jack the ripper…..

MY FRIEND DEATH

I talked with death, in midst of life
We walked together, hand in hand
As friends conversed, twixt day and night
As moonlight washed upon the sand

A pact we made upon that shore
A life of meaning, I should make
My health he then did fully restore
But warned me, that my heart would break

And so through life as lovers lost
All love affairs have come to naught
Loneliness a sunken cost
Solitude and depth in thought

In later life now grey and lined
I gaze upon this sea of glass
A grain of sand, the time has refined
Knowing soon to breathe my last

As I sit astride the golden dunes
And write my poems faithfully
Of epic sonnets, varied tunes
Flow streams of words up for display

And when should come that fateful day
The reaper calls to scythe my soul
This legacy I hope will stay
When into those murky depths we stroll

As I sink beneath the waves
My body stiff, demeanour cold
Think of the sacrifices made
To scribe as this legacy unfolds

In deaths caress, I shall embrace
A tranquil smile upon my face

A TALE FROM THE CRYPT

Overcame with dread this night
As the church bell tolled it peeled midnight
The twelfth peel had such an eerie tone
Lingered long an echo droned

Through the gate I shyly trod
With a limping gait, traversed the sod
Of freshly dug graves to bury the dead
Holes laid bare the diggers fled

Moon s halo dimmed by long black clouds
Obscuring stars no light around
Black as pitch and thick as tar
No torch to shine I can't see far

Just feel my way across the graves
The headstones cracked and broken staves
Rusted gates and panel work
Overgrown bushes where the darkness lurked

Eyes watching from the trees
And the gargoyles in the eaves
Of the ruined church with doors nailed shut
No worship here just decay and rot

Hairs stand on end, that electric feel
Pit of the stomach, cramping so real
Somethings lurking in the night
Just out of reach and out of sight

No light to see no one to call
This blackness allows no shadow fall
The hooting owl beats its wings
As bats acrobat on invisible strings

Mist and fog, bring a heavy damp
Like a liquid curtain as I tramp
And trudge my way to the furthest crypt
Its memorial offerings torn and ripped

A low pitched growl and heavy breath
Sets my teeth on edge with thoughts of death
Of nocturnal monsters and beasts from myth
Or serial killers escaped here with

Bad intent to do their worst
Or stumbling into a witches curse
Or what of zombies straight from the clay

Could have risen from those graves today

Could be lurking behind any tomb
Or behind the doors in the catacombs
This foreboding I cannot dispel
Of a reaping time a date with hell

An apocalypse, released with ease
War, famine, pestilence, disease
All the horsemen come to call
In this lonely church yard I suddenly fall

I bang my head on the concrete slab
Think of Frankenstein's monster in the lab
Blood drips down from my forehead
Did that stone slab move is it a bed

For a vampire lover smelling blood
A thirsty longing to drink she could
Easily overpower my will
And drink me dry, whilst I laid still

If I have to die of this wretched curse
A vampires kiss what could be worse
Than appearing again, night after night
Stalking people, tasting their fright

In the steel tainted blood of industrial folk
Their sounds stifled in their throat
As their bodies go strangely loose
The sanguine taste as I am perfused

With blood so black, like a midnight flower
But infused with life it gives such power
Allows me to see into the night
A clarity of vision, as in daylight

But now I feel the heat of dawn
Seek the crypt where I was born
And there I lay my head to sleep
Definitely not praying, no soul to keep

RE WITCHED

By hunter's moon, my night began
As the mist swirled, with grey fingers
The graveyard gates closed with a clang
And fresh earth smell still lingers

The owl, the bat, the mouse, the cat
All nocturnal creatures roving
Upon the tomb where I am sat
A feeling of foreboding
Why am I here it may not be clear
I am a vampire killer
We're here at three, my witch and me
In this urban graveyard thriller

Now remember this a rare old twist
I too am a vampire
In this very graveyard, I was turned
By an old flame of my desire

I then recall, that werewolf brawl
When my maker's throat was ravaged
And then my quest, which as you guessed
Was to hunt every werewolf savage

But to my surprise, as the bodies did rise
I met a she-wolf so wanton
We made love with the stars above
With wild and free abandon

But to my shock, a vampire knocked
Upon our woodland cabin
She let him stay, but he had his way
Then promptly caved her head in

And so today, my vigil holds sway
Until I kill this creature
This witch and I so patiently
A horror double feature

Then I saw that beast before
He had a chance to spy on me
I'll part his head with a sword I said
No matter who decried me?

My witches spell it kept me well
While I quickly slew this demon
And now I wait for dawn's first rays
To kiss me so I'll move on

TO THE HANGING TREE

Sat, in reflection, the dark moon stares down
Looking at me with a scolding frown
Nothing I've done deserves such contempt
I've prayed to the lord and tried to repent

They caught me killing for food, this is true
Couldn't stay hungry, so I poached game in lieu
Of slave labour for a crust of dry bread
By the end of this night, I know I'll be dead

Sentenced to hang at the old gallows tree
A dawn execution, then I guess I'll be free
Stare at these sandstone walls in my cell
I fear that my family may suffer as well

As dawn approaches the key turns in the lock
The jailer arrives with a rope and sackcloth
Binds my hands and offers me the sack
I whisper, "No thank you" and hand it him back

I will see my accusers in the hour of my death
They'll be forever cursed by my dying breath
If there's any justice beyond this grim life
I'll be back to haunt them for the rest of their lives

Now face the long walk, to the hanging wood
From the castle dungeons, I helped to make good
Past the pious old church, that gave me no grace
Down endless stone steps, at a cumbersome pace

My prayers were ignored and my pleas were rebuffed
The justice dispensed is exceedingly rough
But now to my death I solemnly walk
As villagers stand by to jeer and hawk

To the hangman noose, I duly arrive
Never a chance that I will survive
Hopefully, immediately, my neck will just break
The thought of a struggle for breath, a mistake
Think of the good times family have had
Don't dwell on the bad, nor be terribly sad
Soon my life's end, on which I won't dwell
Will lead to great suffering, I'll give them all hell

Stood at the base of the hanging oak
Platform removed but my neck never broke
Strangling and staring at malevolent eyes
I swore retribution, I cursed, and then I died

NO STATELY GHOST

Let me paint you a picture, set you a scene
On this blustery blood moon night
A wuthering hillside, wind biting and keen
Moon cloud bound and hidden from sight

Rain falls in sheets, pounding the walls
The church and the castle alike
In the roaring black night, a screech owl calls
As the tower bell strikes the last chime, of midnight

A poacher was I hung in the wood
For a pheasant, for the family to eat
I swore retribution, a curse if I could
Wreak revenge on whomever I meet

They buried me somewhere out in the woods
No hallowed ground for criminal, they said
Now I've returned as I'd hoped I would
A spirit intent on unbridled revenge

The gravestones of marble, granite, and stone
Run wet with the deluge, in this miserable place
Freshly dug graves, diggers long gone
I'll find new owners, for their space

Found with my wrath, I can move earthly objects
Float straight through windows, through walls, or locked doors
Now is the time to encumber my subjects
Haunt them profusely, never a pause

Start with the canon, that pious, tonsured prude
No absolution from heaven for me!
In face high and mighty, he was decidedly rude
At the base of my oak hanging tree

Find him inside, with his prayer book in hand
Dim candlelight dances its shadows and light
Hourglass turned, hear the running of the sand
When the last grain has landed, I'll end him tonight

As a vengeful spectre, my rage gives me substance
A shimmering form, amorphous and hazy
That silly old fool gets, glimpsed me perchance
Trembles with fear, eyes frantic and crazy
Pick up a revered cross from the mantle
Silver and sharp base heavy and blunt
Praying to god, this worm spouts and rattles
As I cave in his head, with the base at the front

Carl Butler

Gained my first victim, the blood moon appears
Darkens in sympathy, for the red river running
Satiated feeling, my form disappears
I'll plan my next killing, with such ghostly cunning

This first revenge taken was too quick to end
But this cassocked canon was merely a fool
My next sorry target will know unending revenge
For he passed the sentence when I broke the rules

 And so as bats play and owls scour the hillside
The wind howls, the trees roar, the village is asleep
I return to my rest, for a while by my graveside
And dream of revenge and appointments to keep

NOX SPECTRUM

Actions born of desperation, retribution born of injustice
Revenge born of wrath, extreme behaviour born of hate
Madness born of eternal despair
The cold pre-dawn mist curls like grasping hands around the graveyard
The final hoot of the owl gives way, to the crow of the cock
My spectred self dissipates, like a mist on the wind

I languish in the anguish, of my ghostly display
I flipped from being the victim to a killer today
My fury bubbled over and the murder was swift
The next one I am waiting for, I'll find a new twist

Tonight, I'll find the magistrate, in his stately home
I'm sure he has a family, they're fairly well known
I plan to haunt his skinny wife and scare her to death
And choke the life out of his son, I'll take his last breath

Once he's put them in the ground, I'll watch his despair
Only then will I appear to him that should give him a scare
I'll reappear and torture him, night after night
To see this worm turn and cringe at me, will be a delight

Whilst awaiting retribution, I will visit my wife
See my loving daughter, as she sleeps through the night
Can't wait to see them, just to check they are well
The last I saw of either, was through the bars of the cell

I find my way to my old house and slip right inside
Only to have my heart ripped out, I discover they've both died
With no one to protect them and provide for their care
Disease and hunger took them both, in a pit of despair

I seek out their gravestones but there's none to be found
A simple wooden cross with a name just thrust in the ground
No kind words of comfort, nor grief, nor remorse
I'm completely devastated, having seen this discourse

But now, my mind turns frantically, what have I done?
Not only have they gone to rest, I can see neither one
Neither ghosts nor spirits, they're just left to rest in peace
Whilst I've been doomed to walk this earth, a killing disease

Yes I'm an apparition, I'm eternally damned
When all my vengeance is finished, there's no more to demand
I'll suffer now, forever, and always be alone
Sobbing by their graveside or haunting our home

So should you ever come here, on a dark and stormy night?
Be careful where you come to call, you may get more than a fright
I've descended into madness and its grip will not relent
I've created my own spirit hell, for which I cannot repent

My afterlife is fearsome, I wail and curse and cry
My heartfelt curse rebounded, when I decided to defy
The call from God in heaven, to simply let my spirit rest
Now all I have is murder and the hauntings I detest

It's clear my action brought me back, to this sorry place
Wrath, despair, and anger are the demons that I face
If only I'd relented and tamed the vicious beast
I'd be lying with my family, where together we would find peace

WHERE SPIRIT'S DWELL

It is not heaven, it is not hell
I've glimpsed the realm where spirits dwell
No white light or rolling bell
Devoid of sight, taste, sound, or smell

Touch only void, night all around
No breath of life or hearts to pound
This labyrinth below the mound
Where shadows hide and make no sound

This purgatory for the dead
Some bleed back through from whence they've fled
Determined ghosts by wrath are led
To haunt this mortal realm instead

A timeless place, absent all grace
The destiny of the human race
Must interrupt this quickened pace
This selfish pride, this mad disgrace

Or before too long, you all will see
This shadow realm to which we flee
Larger than the widest sea
Deeper than any rooted tree

And yet the ghosts who wander still
Upon this earth have had their fill
Pleading, moaning, wailing still
Some go mad, some simply kill

I went to get my family back
After finishing my attacks
Of motion, there's a total lack
Can you discern black on black?

But whilst I am now but a shell
Of the poacher laid within his cell
To reap my vengeance, my soul I did sell
But now I'll stay in the place, where spirits dwell

THE REAPING

Saw vultures in the clouds, last eve
Grey and menacing, poised to feed
Ravens came, disturbing my dream
Withered husks from planted seed

These omens of a troubled mind
Hell bound society, I see the signs
The die is cast, the warrant signed
The disturbing outcome has been designed

And ending to which I'm attuned
Foretold in historic runes
Sung about in ancient tunes
Tales reflected in the moon

Weep quietly this pool of tears
Filled up with drops of haunted fears
Dark depths added through the years
Over which the ghost ship steers

Reaper standing on the prow
Scythe in hand gets ready now
Once in port, he'll be on the prowl
With an ever-present scowl

Seeking souls, to take to hell
Or to the place, that spirits dwell
Thousands fall under his spell
No remorse for those who fell

Time of pestilence and war
Have his minions keeping score
Armageddon! These vows been sworn
Take vengeance on a life of scorn

Creeps upon your soul, with stealth
Trouble breathing, failing health
Low esteem, no sense of self
More concerned with material wealth
Mass hysteria taking flight
Waves of madness in plain sight
A year of lunacy, a season of fright
Complete surrender, no more fight

Reaps his victims, one by one
By silver moon or Monday sun
Takes every mortal soul, bar none
Now his reaping has begun

With his scythe, he scrapes the earth
With this ancient blight, an evil curse
Social gatherings have been dispersed
But relaxing rules just made it worse

Now as you struggle, for your last breath
Your pride and stubbornness failed the test
Or your mental state got so depressed
Death lays his hand upon your chest

BANSHEE

One tear-filled night, at the graveyard site
My love now cold and out of sight
A sudden death, I know not why
I linger here, I stand and cry

The sky joins in the heavens sob
Oh my god! Why have you robbed me, of the only lover's chance I had?
I only ever sought to grab
These fine moments with both hands and live
I had but so much love to give

But now it's buried, in this grave
My heart in splinters. To her I gave
Every loving thought I had
This untimely death drove me mad

Hysterical, I've now become
Unhinged, maybe not going home
Cold and wet, I sit alone
My long lament upon this stone

I cry, wail, weep and moan
For the future, I cannot own
And then, suddenly, I see
Another figure watching me

She almost glides across the path
Her eyes contain, both pain and wrath
Suddenly, her mouth agape
The most astounding sound escapes

The shrillest wail, you'll ever hear
And then stood right by me
This wailing spirit, a real banshee
Of death, she tells and so foretells
Whoever hears her voice, will dwell
On earth no more, after this night
My heart is lifted, I stand here bright

Expectant and no more in pain
Tonight, I will see my love again
I so much long, to gain her back
Suddenly, a heart attack
The wailing ceased

REAPER'S SHOW

From the darkness, I awoke
From the spirit world invoked
Sat here, in this garb of green
I now await, this Halloween

Once the reapers moon is full
And all the hate is at a lull
So with book and scythe in hand
I will reap souls across this land

Through mist ridden, gloomy stand
With my host, at my command
And all my carrion birds
Bring back souls, so long deferred

While the spirits have their fun
My time of reaping has begun
Since before the dawn of man
I had renounced a master plan

My only burning need
To take the souls, on which I feed
I was the chaos from the storm
Before the universe was born

And I will be there at the end
As the final planet dies
And total blackness lies
And only I, and time reside

FOE PLAY

I thought you'd like to come and play
I'm needing company today
I know, I'm seeming rather flirty
I'm desperate, to get down and dirty

I've eyed you up, for many days
I'm feeling horny, so depraved
Meet me in the forest soon
It's about an hour, until the full moon

I'll do for you things, you can't resist
I'll tug and tease, with hands and lips
Take my hand, I'll take you away
You will come for me, under Luna's silver sway

I'll take your hand into the wood
Just take it slow and make it good
Just remember, when you're through
I need to do, the same for you

Into the woods, they strolled away
The guy thought it was his lucky day
And yes he came, but not too soon
For looking on a cold winter moon

Teeth and lips became claws and fangs
That tore and ripped and bit his hands
And back, throat, and more
He bled out quickly on the floor

The blood was spent and carcass rent
This poor guy sure came and went
But well deserved his erstwhile fate
For the previous women, he had raped

This raven girl, shape-shifting wolf
Took his seed then just engulfed
His manhood simply disappeared
Animal attacks will now be feared
But in this woodland by the village
Retribution! Was a she-wolf bitch?

MOON CURSE

The harvest moon has come too soon
I can feel her tug, her pull my doom
Quicksilver bright from behind a cloud
My heart beats faster, sweat on my brow

My god! What an intense pain...
Damn, oh no! There it goes again
Like my soul, is sucked out by a straw
My skins on fire, I'm wearing raw

The cramps begin, then to my knees
To the heavens, "Help me please!"
But if God is watching, he formed this curse
Now this pain is getting worse

My bones now crack, I yell and scream
My tears are running down in streams
I arch my back and still, I moan
Now hair grows, more, than I have known

Brown and thick from head to toe
Now claws appear and so I go
Scream in pain, then suddenly
I hear a howl emanate from me

With protruding nose and pointed teeth
My mouth is dripping underneath
A sense of smell that heightened stench
As the last bones in my body, reset and wrench

On all fours now, I pad and bound
My pointed ears hear every sound
Its bible black, yet still I see
Right through this forests nocturnal frieze

Now it is, of that I'm sure
I am a werewolf and there is no cure

RAVEN HEART

Through Cimmerian woods, I trudged today
To seek your ravenesque display
You corvid bird of prophecy
The spirited glimpses that you see

Obsidian plumage with a satin sheen
I seek the knowledge that you've seen
These carrion offerings, I will bestow
To glimpse the future, I would know

Speak to me, oh wizened bird
You remember faces, undeterred
Those anthracite beads, stare right through me
As you are sitting comfortably?

Of Odin's power, in myth you're blessed
The spirits come at your behest
Your darkened plumage and strength of frame
Rivals hawks in all but name

The sinister naming, of your kith and kin
That band together, in original sin
Blot out the sun, when together they fly
The murder of crows goes swiftly by

That sun descended, behind leaden clouds
As your tenor voice, calls long and loud
Called the name I once revered
The prophecy is now quite clear

The loss you forecast I'll forswear
To learn the magic hidden there
Of psych pomp, make me aware
Of your second sight and fell despair

Insidious seer of the dark
Upon your journey, I'll now embark
Incarnate now, my soul will be
Chained to evil eternally

I am your apprentice and your muse
Upon this darkened path I choose
Magic's darkly under-toned
This journey now I'll take alone

THE CARD GAME

My time machine, so sharp and keen
Against the window, pain is seen
As raindrops spatter in between
The flashing neon's sequenced scene
I'm whisked back, a century or more
The Mississippi rivers lore
And paddle steamers, brash and loud
Whose huge paddle wheels standing proud

Lit up, with the light fantastic
Would steam along, that river frantic
Gamblers all would come to stay
Try their luck, at cards they'd play
Or wheel roulette, or on the go
Watching the latest can-can show
Leggy girls with tattered thighs
Frilly knickers, kicking high

Giving it some Oooh La La
Drinking liquor at the bar
Now thrust into this southern scene
Comes a gambler, fierce and mean
With his six-gun polished clean
The showboat gets up a head of steam
Let the poker game begin
And let the bravest gambler win

The poker table set for six
The stack of chips marked 666
The devil's game was played tonight
We play for souls, from dusk till light
A vampire, witch, gunman, and me
The dealer and the voodoo queen
What a quite outlandish scene
The weirdest bunch, you've ever seen

But this game was deadly rough
Your poker chips were not enough
Your soul bought you passage to this game
Collect it, if you win the game
If you lost during the night
You'd forfeit any human right
Become a vampire or a ghoul
Or mindless zombie, not so cool

Maybe a familiar face
A witch's cat, in the rat race
Did I mention the card dealer?

It was of course the grim reaper
He plays to win, don't hold your breath
You may be good, but can't cheat death
The 4 horsemen watched, true to form
These scary riders, on the storm

With this game now underway
Will a full house win the day?
Or what about a royal flush?
That red river run, makes the vampire blush
The witches' straight cards, all jet black
Then my 4 aces, back to back
The gunslinger, now cactus jack
Got upset, he lost the pack

Stood up, drew, and went to fire
Death decided he should retire
Ripped the heart right from his chest
Blood ran through his Sunday best
Now, from six, were down to five
But no one here gets out alive
The poker game goes round on round
Suddenly, the witch screams loud

She's now lost her demon hold
Her fires gone out, the cauldrons cold
Fancy that, she's in a spin that last hand the vampire wins
Now death declares, it's time to die
Watch that witch to hades fly
The vampire, me, and voodoo queen
Are left in this midnight scene
Next hand, is all mine to show

Time to make old queenie go
With the scythe stood at his side
The reaper s death slice, side to side
Cuts the voodoo queen in 2
Now, vampire, it's me and you!
You may be black, but I'm all red
You can't be killed, already dead
But now, this makes you laugh the most

I am a shade, a gambling ghost
And just then the clock strikes 6
The sun shines in, the vampires tricked
Fried right up, burnt to a crisp
I am the winner, my chains I slip
Bound no more, to go to hell
I'm free to go, where spirits dwell
That separate tale, I'll later tell

That place neither heaven nor is it hell
Suffice to say not all bodes well
But for now, my, soul is back from hell

FAIRYTALE

I am the nightmare behind the legends
The darkness behind the veil
The reason for the caution
Behind the fairy-tale

I linger in the shadows
Sinister and calm
Breathing down your neck at night
I mean you all great harm

I don't hide in your closet
Nor lay beneath your bed
I whisper all my demon deeds
Straight into your head

Go on just taste that apple
That wolf just wants to play
I've just found the perfect house
Where granny loves to stay

I will seed your deepest fears
And grow them like a tree
Until those limbs wrap around your heart
So you are never free
Now then just remember
Always, I'll prevail!
I'm the reason for your nightmares
And the cause of fairy-tales

SINISTER

The sun cares not if it blinds your vision
The moon doesn't blink, when it pulls you in
The breeze has no mercy, in its cold derision
As your miserable bones creak, under the weight of your skin

The wind strips you bare, till you're standing quite naked
The sea rubbing salt into lacklustre eyes
The fire burns you black, till you look over baked
Then wood turns to ash that must be a painful surprise!

The earth steals your breath, in the dark, you are buried
Like mushrooms or fungus, trapped in the soil
To dig your way out, your hands redraw and bloodied
Yet still no reward, for those hard years of heart-breaking toil

Life is a bitch but at least you're still breathing
Sometimes nature's way is to hurry your leaving

BLACK SWAN EVOLUTION

I am the evolution
I am what is meant to be
I am the black swan's mate
Your ink has set me free

I have risen from the ashes
I am the aftermath
I am now endemic
A dark and stormy path

I am what will come to pass
I am no compromise
You will learn to worship me
A goddess in disguise

I shall touch the heavens
I shall conquer hell
I shall rule the shadowlands
The place where poets dwell

I am reincarnation
A sequel given birth
Look for me in earnest
Where chaos struck the earth

I am my raison d'etre
I simply came to be
When you read my verses
I hope they set you free

AFTERWORD

Thank you for sharing my journey through nature and a vast range of emotions.

Having written over 1600 poems encompassing many genres, I think I have represented well a selection in this first book and have evolved as a writer considerably, over the past 12 months.

As we emerge from lockdown it is all too easy to forget this BLACK SWAN event. Remember today is for living, tomorrow? Well that's for the birds....

ACKNOWLEDGEMENTS

So many people and things have influenced the last year, Mother Nature for sure.

The Black Swan I caught sight of 12 months ago. My muse, the metaphorical moon.

But seriously, the poetry group Dark Poetry Society, for its support and unique perspective on poetry, Amanda Jayne Benton, fellow group owner & friend, for seeing the poet buried beneath the beard and proof reading my work, a real inspiration on my journey.

Charles Cooper for his patience in formatting and working with the manuscript.

And my children Richard, Jason, Shane, & Kathryn.

And to all who have seen and supported my poetry along the way.

Thank you all!

BIO

Affectionately known as Father Nature due to his key genre of writing nature poetry.

Carl is 57, single, living in a leafy Cheshire suburb. He is co-owner of a successful poetry group on Facebook, enjoys nature, walks and the simple things in life.

CPSIA information can be obtained
at www.ICGtesting.com
Printed in the USA
BVHW040106070921
616157BV00014B/299